Canon EOS R6 II User Companion

Your Indispensable Handbook with Illustrations to Master the EOS R6 II

By

Mats Sauer

Table of Content

INTRODUCTION

The Canon EOS R6 II is a high-performance full-frame mirrorless camera that offers a versatile set of features for both still photography and videography. It features a 24.2MP CMOS sensor, DIGIC X image processor, and 5-axis image stabilization, which can help to produce sharp images and videos even in low-light conditions. The R6 II also has a fast and accurate autofocus system, which can track subjects even in fast-moving or challenging situations.

In addition to its impressive still photography capabilities, the R6 II also offers a variety of features for video recording. It can record 4K video at up to 60fps, and it also has a built-in microphone and headphone jack. The R6 II also supports Canon's Dual Pixel CMOS AF technology, which provides smooth and accurate autofocus during video recording.

The Canon EOS R6 II is a powerful and versatile camera that is suitable for a wide range of photographers and videographers. It is a great choice for sports, wildlife, and event photographers, as well as for those who want to create high-quality video content.

The Canon EOS R6 II is a powerful and versatile camera that is suitable for a wide range of photographers and videographers. It offers excellent performance in both still photography and videography, and it is well-designed and comfortable to use. If you are looking for a high-performance mirrorless camera that can do it all, the Canon EOS R6 II is a great option. This user guide will help you get the most out of this camera and fully maximize all of its features.

CHAPTER 1: GETTING THE CAMERA UP AND RUNNING

Preparing the Camera for Initial Use

Setting up your camera is quick and straightforward. You must charge the battery, attach a lens, adjust the viewfinder, insert and format a memory card, and make a few settings. If you've used a previous EOS model, it's even easier as you already know what to do. If you're new to Canon or digital SLR cameras, don't worry; I'll give you some extra information to help you.

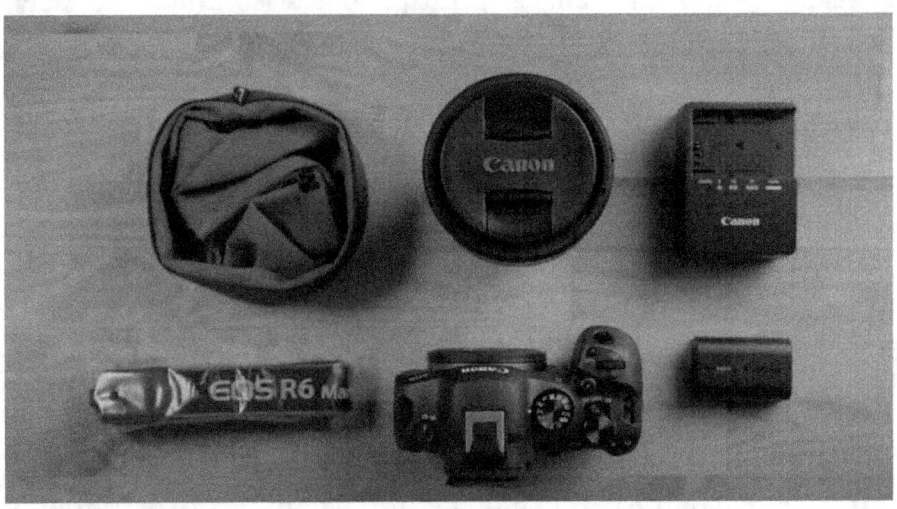

Power Options

Your Canon EOS R6 II is a complex equipment requiring a charged battery. To get started, charge the LP-E6NH lithium-ion battery pack with your camera. A fully charged battery can give you around 400 shots, depending on whether you use the LCD or viewfinder for composing shots. Remember that rechargeable batteries lose some charge over time, even when not in use, due to a chemical reaction. So, the battery that came with your camera may have lost some power and should be recharged before going out for extensive photography.

Your camera has different battery chargers, but most people prefer the compact LC-E6 charger. If you buy one of the optional chargers, you get extra features and a backup charger to keep your camera powered until you can replace the main one. It's handy to have an extra charger if the original one breaks or you need to charge multiple batteries simultaneously, especially with the BG-R10 grip.

Here are your power options:

- **LC-E6:** It is the standard charger for the camera, and it works with older models that use LC-E6 or LC-E6N batteries. It's very convenient because it's small, has built-in wall plug prongs, and can be connected directly to your power strip or wall socket without a cord.

- **LC-E6E:** It is like LC-E6 but needs a cord to charge a single battery. It can be helpful when the power outlet is hard to reach. You can plug in the cord and place the charger on your desk or in a more convenient spot. The cord is standard and works with many chargers and devices. So, I bought multiple cords and kept them plugged into different walls. I can connect my camera charger, laptop charger, and other electronic components to these cords without crawling around behind furniture. The cord doesn't use any power when not plugged into a charger. Remember to unhook the charger from the cord when not charging your batteries.

- **Car Battery Cable CBC-E6:** This is a simple accessory that connects to your car's lighter or accessory socket. It lets you use your camera's battery to shoot in remote places without AC power.

- **Battery Grip BG-R10:** This is a $375 add-on that can hold one or two LC-E6NH batteries. It can double your camera's shooting capacity and provides extra controls for vertical shooting. It also includes a power adapter for charging LP-E6NH batteries while they are in the camera.

- **USB Power Adapter PD-E1:** The USB Power Adapter PD-E1 costs about $200 and allows you to charge LPE6NH batteries without taking them out of the camera or grip. You can charge the batteries with a cheaper adapter or power brick if it can provide more than 5V and has a USB-C output. Regular USB chargers might not work and could show an error message. In that case, you can turn off the camera and remove the battery for a few minutes to clear the error.

The small light at the bottom right of the camera's back will glow green while it's charging. This light also flashes red when the camera saves photos to the memory card. Once charging is done, the light turns off.

- **AC Adapter Kit ACK-E6:** The AC Adapter Kit ACK-E6 lets you power your camera directly from an electrical outlet, so you don't need to use the camera's battery. Studio photographers find this useful because they take many pictures for extended periods and need a constant and reliable power source. You can connect the camera to a flash sync cord or radio device and the studio flash to power packs or AC power. It's also handy for viewing images on a TV connected to your camera, shooting video, or capturing remote or time-lapse photos.

Charging the Battery

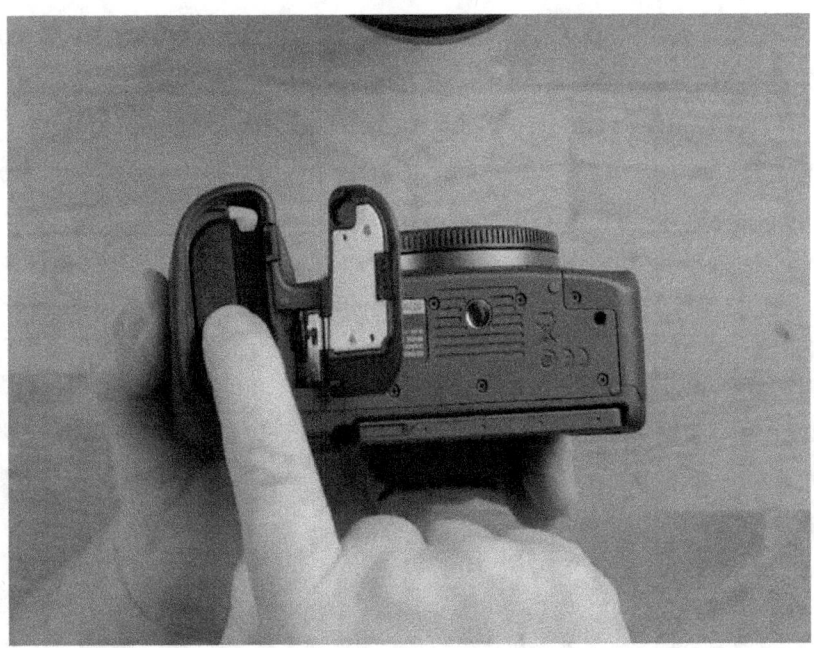

A light starts flashing when you put the battery into the LC-E6 charger. The flashing continues until the battery is 50% charged, then it blinks between 50% and 75% charged in sets of two. After that, it blinks in sets of three until it reaches 90% charge, which usually takes about 90 minutes. To be safe, you should let the charger continue for around 60 more minutes until the status lamp turns steady green to ensure a full charge. Once the battery is fully charged, you can insert it into the camera by flipping the lever on the bottom. Just press the white retaining button to remove the battery from the camera.

Mounting a Lens

When you want to attach a lens to your camera, protect your equipment and avoid dust. If your camera has no lens on it, choose the lens you want to use and loosen the back lens cap without obliterating it. Then, place the lens vertically in your camera bag's slot so it stays safe and easily accessible. By loosening the back lens cap, you can quickly remove it right before attaching it, keeping the lens's rear element covered until then.

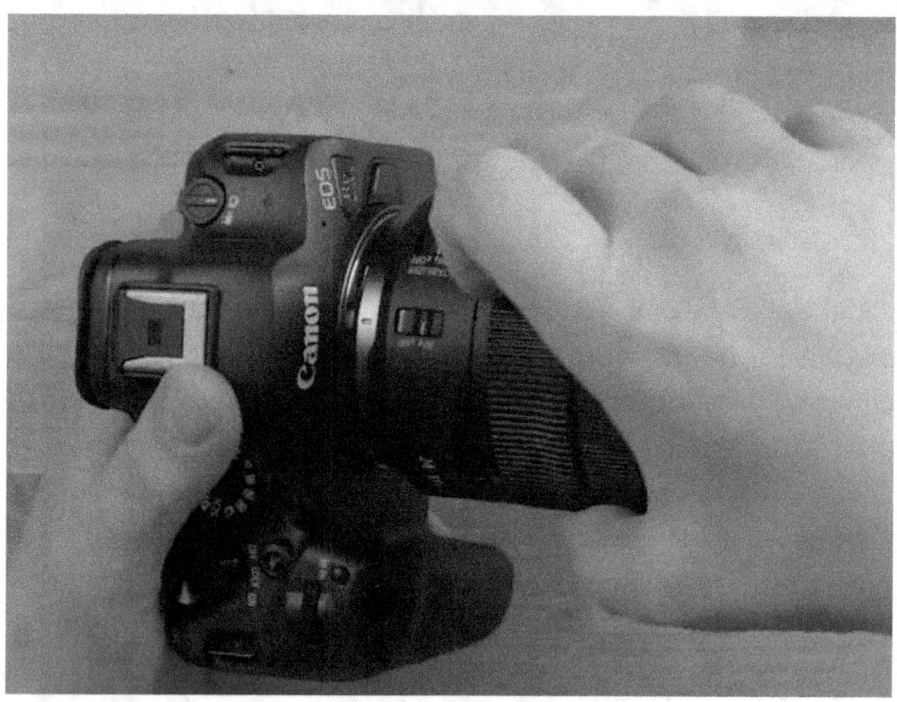

First, twist the body cap to take it off the camera. Always use the body cap when there's no lens on the camera to keep dust out. Dust can settle inside the camera and reach the sensor, so it's better to have less dust inside. If you're not careful, the body cap also protects the sensor from getting damaged by objects, including your fingers.

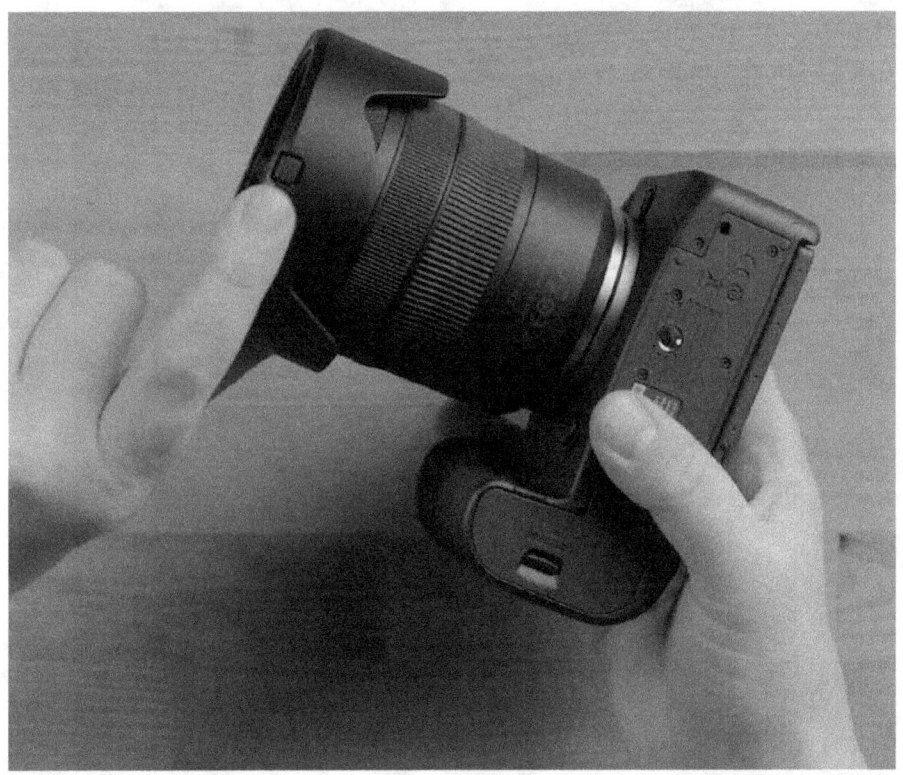

First, remove the body cap from the camera. Then, please remove the rear lens cap from the lens and keep it aside. Next, attach the lens to the camera by aligning the red marks on the barrel and the lens mount. Rotate the lens gently until it fits securely in place. Switch the focus mode on the lens to autofocus (AF) and turn on the stabilizer switch. If the lens hood is attached in a reversed position for transportation, twist it off and put it back facing outward. The lens hood helps

13

protect the lens from accidental bumps and fingerprints and reduces flare caused by extra light.

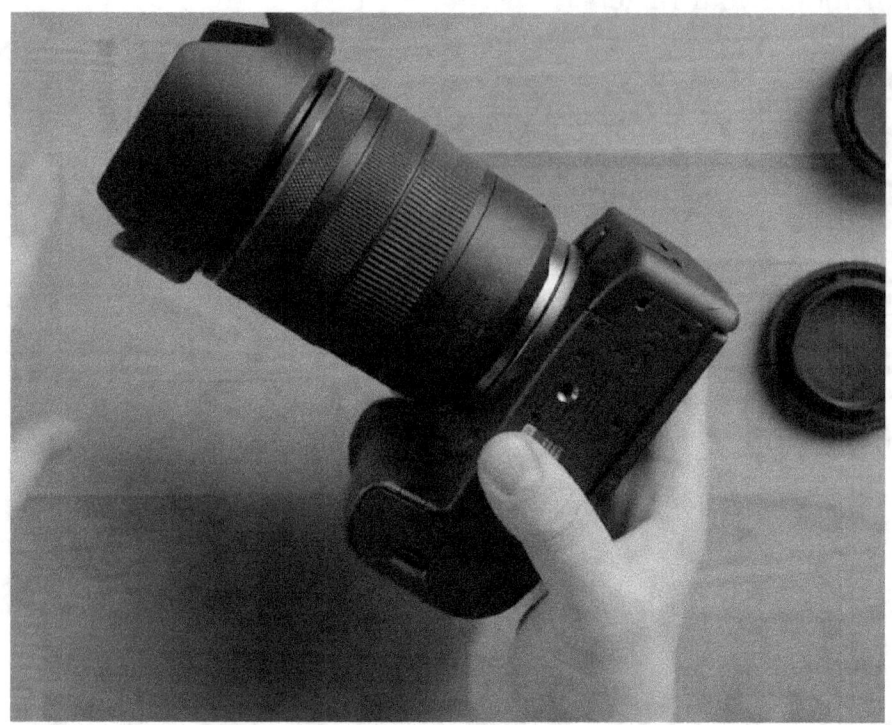

Adjusting Diopter Correction

If your eyesight isn't perfect, you might need help seeing clearly through the camera's viewfinder. If you wear glasses, you can use the camera's built-in diopter adjustment, which allows you to make the viewfinder look sharp without wearing your glasses.

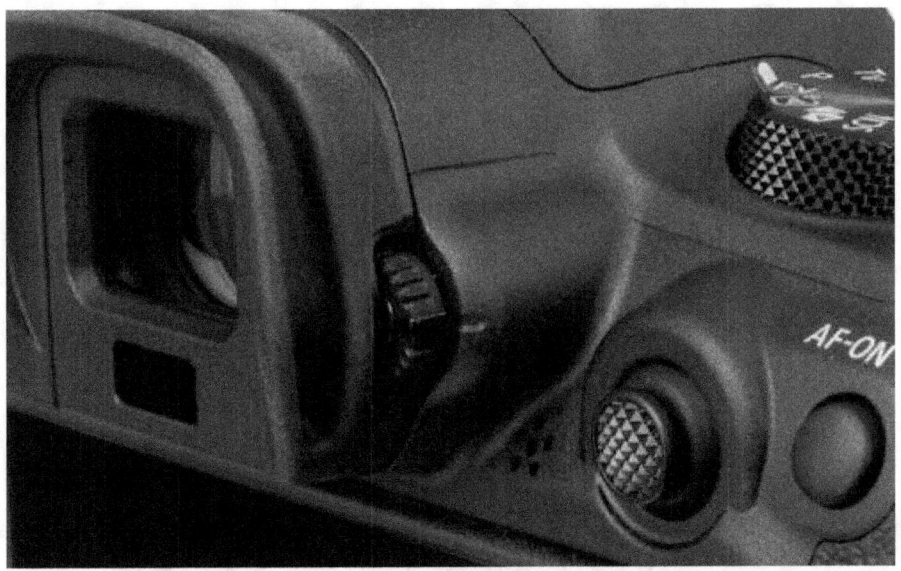

To do this, turn the diopter adjustment control on the viewfinder's right side until the display looks clear to you. The adjustment range is from -4 to +2.

Inserting a Memory Card

You need to put a memory card inside to take photos with your camera. Here's how you do it:

- Make sure the camera is switched off before you remove the memory card. The camera will remind you if you try to open the memory card slot while it's still writing photos to the card.

- On the camera's right side, slide the door toward the back to release and open the cover.

- Take your memory card and insert it into either of the two slots. The label on the memory card should face the back of the camera. Make sure the edge with the metal contacts goes into the slot first.

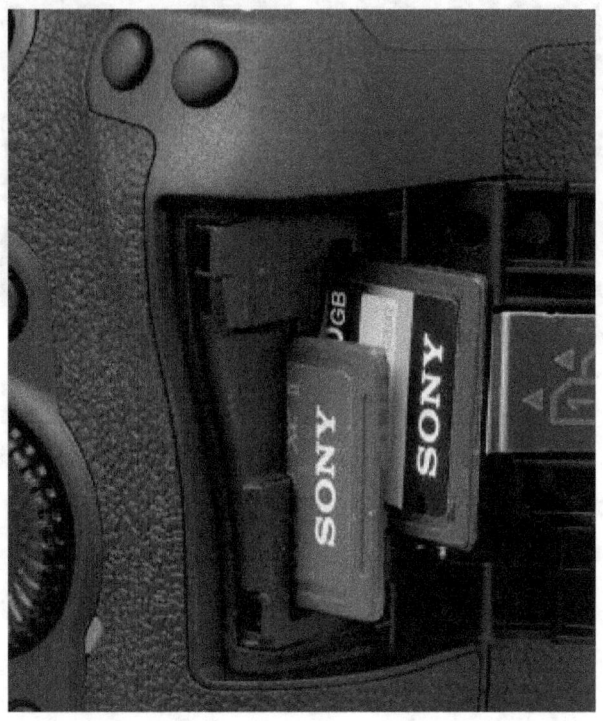

There are two slots available: Slot 1 is closest to the back of the camera, and Slot 2 is behind it. Both of them support UHS-II-compatible SD cards.

If you put in just one memory card, the camera will use it without problems. I'll explain how to choose which card is used when two cards are inserted. After closing the card door, your preflight checklist is complete! Remember, when you are ready

16

to take a picture, remove the lens cap. Take out a memory card later, press it down, and it will pop out.

It's essential to consider an early issue with the original EOS R and EOS RP cameras: they had only one card slot. Professional or semi-professional cameras, which usually cost $2,000 or more, should have the option to use two card slots for backup or extra storage. People who used cameras with single film rolls in the past were less bothered by this because they used multiple cameras during a shoot for backup and overflow.

Newer models, such as the R6 II, have a solution to the problem - they have two slots for memory cards. It is useful for photojournalists covering breaking news or sports, as they can quickly switch to a fresh card when one gets almost full. But for regular use, they usually save images on their fastest or largest memory card and use the second slot as a backup option.

Like the latest SDXC cards, SD cards can quickly transfer data, up to 300 megabytes per second. However, it's essential to know that different brands use various ways to describe their speeds. Write speed is how fast the card saves an image, and read speed is how fast the card sends the image to your computer through a fast connection like a USB 3.x card reader.

Exploring External Camera Features

Topside controls

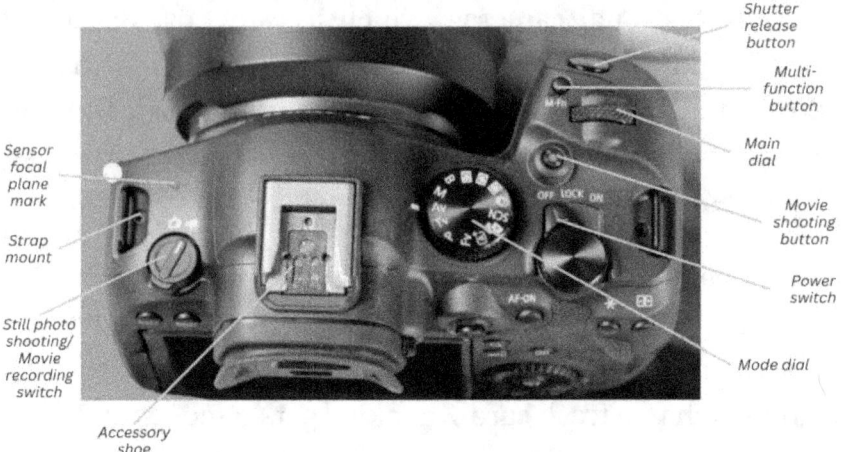

- **Zoom scale:** It shows how much you have zoomed in or out. (Only available on zoom lenses!)

- **Zoom lock:** When the zoom is at its widest position, you can use this switch to keep it locked there. It prevents the lens from accidentally zooming in when pointed downward.

- **Shutter release button:** Press it halfway to lock in the exposure and focus. Press it all the way to take a picture. If the camera has turned off the auto-exposure and autofocus, tapping this button will reactivate both. Also, when you see a review image on the back-panel color

18

LCD, tapping this button will remove the image from the display and reactivate the autoexposure and autofocus.

- **The M-Fn button has two uses:**

To access dial functions, press the button, and a list of available functions will appear horizontally. These functions are displayed in pairs. The preset combinations are:

- o Brightness adjustment and sensitivity setting

- o Image style and focus area

- o Color balance and metering mode

- o Shooting mode and focus operation

When you select a function, you can use the Main dial to change the settings for the top part and the QCD-1 to change the settings for the bottom part. If you want different functions, you can add or remove them. To choose the autofocus area, press the AF point selection button on the upper-right corner of the back of the camera. You can customize this button to have many other functions.

The main dial is used for many shooting settings. When settings come in pairs, like shutter speed and aperture in Manual shooting mode, the main dial is used for one setting (for example, shutter speed), while the QCD-1 is used for the other setting (aperture). During playback of images, the main dial helps you skip a certain number of images, like 1, 10, or 100 images, or jump by date or screen (thumbnails in Index mode), date, or folder. It is also used to move among tabs in the MENU and change settings with the QCD-1 in some menus.

- **Movie shooting button:** Press this button to start recording a video, and press it again to stop recording. You can customize this button to do 40 other functions.

- **Power switch:** Turn the camera on by rotating it to the far right and turn it off by rotating it to the far left. The camera is in the middle Lock position, but specific controls can be frozen to prevent accidental changes. To unlock those controls, move from the Lock position. You can lock specific controls like the Main dial, QCD-1, QCD-2, multi-controller, control ring, or touchscreen panel using the Multi-Function Lock entry in the Set-up 5 menu.

- **Accessory shoe:** The shoe is a place on the camera where you can attach an external flash when you need more light. It allows the flash and the camera to communicate and share information.

- **Sensor focal plane mark:** The symbol on the side of the pentaprism shows where the sensor's focal plane is. It is helpful for precise macro and scientific photography.

- **Strap mount:** You can attach a neck strap to this mount on one side of the camera, and there's a matching mount on the other side to secure the strap.

- **Mode dial:** You can rotate the dial to choose different exposure modes and camera user settings.

Front features

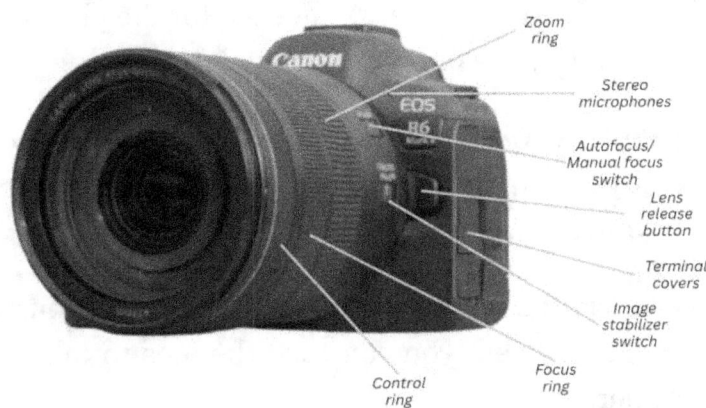

- **Shutter release button:** On the top of the hand grip is a button called the shutter release button. Pressing this button halfway will lock the exposure and focus when using One-Shot mode and Servo AF modes with still subjects.

- **AF-assist beam/Self-timer lamp:** This small light blinks when it helps the camera focus better. It also blinks when you set a timer to show when the photo will be taken.

- **DC coupler cord hole:** This cover near the hand grip opens so you can connect the DC power cable to the camera through the battery compartment.

- **Hand grip:** This helps you hold the camera comfortably and its battery.

- **Depth-of-field preview button:** When you press it, the lens closes to the size needed for the photo, showing how blurry the background will be.

- **Lens mount:** This strong part at the back of the camera lets you attach lenses or accessories using a matching bayonet.

- **Lens release button:** Hold down the button to unlock the lens. Then, you can turn the lens to take it off the camera.

- **Lens lock pin:** When you press and hold the release button, the pin on the lens flange goes back to unlock the lens.

- **RF lens mount index:** Match the mark on your lens with the red notch on the camera's barrel while attaching it.

- **Shutter:** When the camera is turned off, the shutter is closed to protect the sensitive sensor, especially when changing lenses. When you turn the camera on, the shutter opens, so remember to turn it off when swapping lenses. When manually cleaning the sensor, it would help if you only had the shutter open without a lens.

- **Electronic contacts:** These contacts connect to specific points on the lens so that the camera and lens can talk to each other using electronics.

- **Stereo microphones:** The R6 II camera has two on the front, above the lens mount. On the camera's side, you'll find additional controls. Remember that not all lenses have the same features; for example, non-zoom "prime" lenses won't have a zoom ring. The main elements of the camera are as follows: [needs more context to complete the list]

- **Lens hood bayonet:** Canon makes lens hoods for each lens, which attach to the front. The hood's purpose is to block unwanted light from entering the lens, which can cause problems with the image. Always use a lens hood when taking photos to protect the lens from damage. On the other hand, filters can be fragile and are best used to add a specific effect when working in wet or dusty conditions. Lens hoods are a safer option, as they won't break into sharp pieces like filters can.

- **Lens hood alignment mark:** Match the indicator on your lens hood with the right spot, then turn the hood to attach it firmly to the front of your lens.

- **Control ring:** This amazing feature can be set up to control things like how much light the camera lets in, how long the picture is taken for, how sensitive the camera is to light, and how bright or dark the photo should be, as I'll explain in Chapter 14.

- **Focus ring:** Turn the ring to adjust the focus manually or make small adjustments to autofocus.

- **Zoom ring:** Rotate the ring to make things look bigger or smaller.

- **Image stabilizer switch:** This switch controls image stabilization. If your camera is on a tripod, you should turn it off.

- **Autofocus/Manual focus switch:** Canon autofocus lenses have a button that lets you switch between automatic and manual focus.

- **Terminal covers:** The camera's ports and terminals are hidden behind rubber covers to protect them from dust and moisture.

Your camera has different terminals or ports under its covers:

- **USB Type-C digital terminal** lets you transfer photos to your computer using the provided USB cable. You can also use it with the Wireless File Transmitter WFT-E7 II and GPS Receiver GP-E2.

- **HDMI mini OUT terminal:** You can connect your camera to an HDMI-compatible television, video recorder, or other device with an accessory cable (not included with the camera). If you have a high-resolution TV, it's worth getting a Type A to Type D HDMI cable to view your camera's output in full quality. However, please note that the camera's HDMI output doesn't support the CEC (Consumer Electronics Control) protocol for device control.

- **Headphone terminal:** Plug your headphones or other audio devices with a small plug here.

- **Remote control terminal:** You can connect a wired remote control to this spot.

- **External microphone IN terminal:** If you want an external microphone instead of the built-in one for recording sound, plug it in here using a small plug.

Back-of-the-body controls

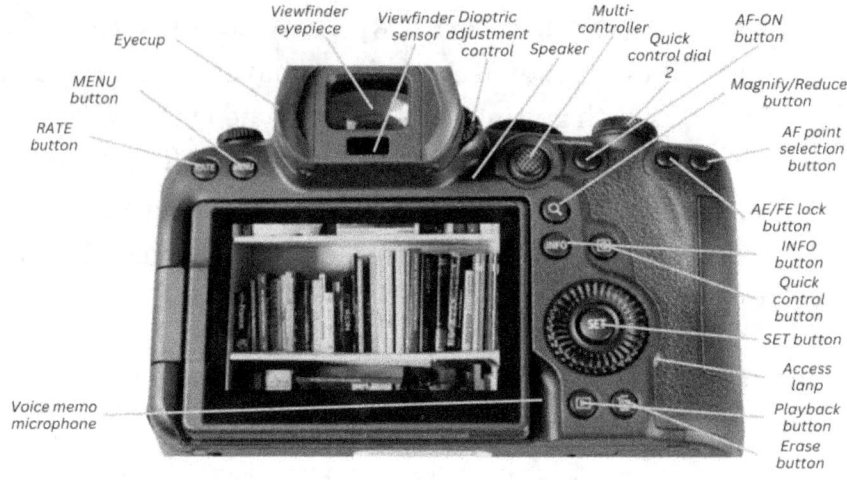

- **MENU button:** This button displays the camera's menu on the screen. It helps you navigate through different settings and options. In a submenu, pressing this button also takes you back to the main menu.

- **RATE button:** By default, this button rates images during playback. You can give images one to five-star or clear ratings by pressing it multiple times. However, you can change its function to assign features like Protect or Erase Images. Also, you can program the button to have dual functions, one by simply pressing it and the other by holding it down and rotating the Quick Control dial. These options include Rate/Image Jump and Protect/Image Jump, which allow you to jump to the next image during image review.

- **Dioptric adjustment control:** Turn this dial while looking through the viewfinder to adjust the image according to your vision.

- **Viewfinder eyepiece/eyecup:** Look through the viewfinder eyepiece to frame your shot. It has a soft rubber frame that blocks out extra light when you press your eye against it tightly, and it also protects your eyeglasses from scratches (if you wear them). The R6 II's electronic viewfinder has 3.69 million tiny dots that make up the image you see.

- **Viewfinder sensor:** This sensor detects when your eye (or any object) gets close to the viewfinder eyepiece. By default, the camera switches between the viewfinder and the screen automatically, but you can set it to switch manually through the camera's menu.

- **Quick Control dial 1 (QCD-1):** Use this dial to adjust shooting options like the aperture (f/stop) or exposure compensation value. It also helps you navigate menus and control some functions set with other buttons, like selecting the autofocus point.

- **Quick Control dial 2 (QCD-2):** The second QCD dial lets you quickly jump between major menus, such as Shooting, AF, Playback, Network, Set-up, and Custom Function menus, without going through each tab. Rotate the Main dial near the shutter release button to move between these menus.

- **AF-ON button:** Press this button to activate the autofocus system without pressing the shutter release halfway. Using this button and others, you can separately lock exposure and focus. To close the exposure, partially press the shutter release or the AE lock button. To autofocus, partially press the shutter release or press the AF-ON button.

- **AE/FE (autoexposure/flash exposure lock button):** In shooting mode, the AE/FE lock button helps lock the camera's or external flash exposure. When you slightly press the shutter button, it locks the exposure setting, and you'll see a () sign at the lower left of the display. If you want to adjust the exposure while keeping the shutter button partially pressed, press the () button again. When you release the shutter button or take a photo, the exposure lock will be removed. If you want to keep the exposure lock for multiple photos, hold down the (*) button while shooting.

The AF point selection button does two things:

  o It lets you choose different AF area modes like Spot AF, 1-Point AF, Expand Area AF, and Zone AF 1, 2, and 3 by pressing it once and then using the M-Fn button to cycle through the options.

  o It allows you to move the AF point or zone around the frame using the directional controls, except in the Whole Area AF mode.

28

- **Multi-controller:** This joystick-like button can move in eight directions to adjust focus points, zoom areas, navigate menus, and perform other functions. It can also be pressed to activate or confirm settings.

- **Magnify/Reduce button:** This button has different functions for Shooting and Playback modes.

- **Shooting mode:** Press the button once to make the view bigger by 5X, then 10X, and then again to return to the regular size (1X). You can also move the zoomed area using the multi-controller while magnifying the image.

- **Playback mode:** Press the button and let go. Then, turn the QCD-2 to the right to zoom in on a still image with 15 magnification levels from 1X to 10X. To zoom out, rotate the QCD-2 to the left, and you can go back to full-frame mode or view 4, 9, 36, or 100 images at once. To see the currently highlighted image in full-frame view, press SET in any index or magnified view.

- **SET button:** This button is used to select or confirm your choices.

- **Card slot cover:** Push the cover towards the back of the camera to open and access the camera's dual card slots.

- **Quick Control (Q) button:** Press this button to access the Quick Control screen, which lets you use various features while shooting. When viewing images in playback, a different Quick Control screen appears, allowing you to protect or rate images, change the jump method, resize, crop, rotate, or perform other functions. I'll explain more about working with these Quick Control screens later in this chapter.

- **Access lamp:** When the lamp is lit or blinking, it shows that the memory card is being used.

- **Erase button:** In Playback mode, this button deletes the picture you view.

- **Playback button:** This shows the latest image you took.

- **INFO button:** Changes the displayed information in shooting and playback modes. It's also used in specific menu screens to access more details or options.

Working with Memory Cards

You can try out the basic controls I just showed you by preparing a memory card. There are three ways to make a blank memory card for your camera, but two are only partially right. Here are your choices, both correct and incorrect:

Transfer (move) files to your computer: When you move all the pictures from your camera memory card to your computer, the old pictures are deleted, making them empty. However, this method won't delete protected images or identify corrupted parts of the card. To have a completely blank card, it's best to format it each time. The only exception is if you want to keep some protected or unerased images on the card to share with others later.

(Don't) Format in your computer: To properly format your memory card for your camera, you should do it directly in the camera itself, not through your computer's card reader or slot. When you format the card using your computer, it might use a file system that the camera doesn't like. The only time you can format the card with your computer is when it's seriously corrupted and the camera can't format it. In that case, let the computer reformat it first and then attempt to format it again using the camera.

Setup menu format: To format a memory card using the recommended method, do the following:

1. Press the MENU button.

2. Use the Main dial to select the Set-up 1 menu, represented by a wrench icon.

3. Use the QCD-1 on the back of the camera to move down to Format Card within the Set-up 1 menu, then press the SET button in the center.

4. Select the card you want to format, then press SET to confirm.

5. Use the QCD-1 to highlight OK, and press SET again to start the format. Optionally, you can press the Trash

button first for an extra thorough low-level "clean-up" format, especially if the card has been used many times.

CHAPTER 2: MASTERING LIGHT AND COLOR CONTROLS

Continuous Lighting Basics

Continuous lighting is easier to understand and work with compared to electronic flash. However, there are some things you should consider, such as the color temperature of the light and how well it reproduces colors accurately. Color temperature is essential, and while it's relevant to continuous light sources, it tends to have more extreme and unpredictable variations compared to electronic flash, which gives consistent daylight-like illumination.

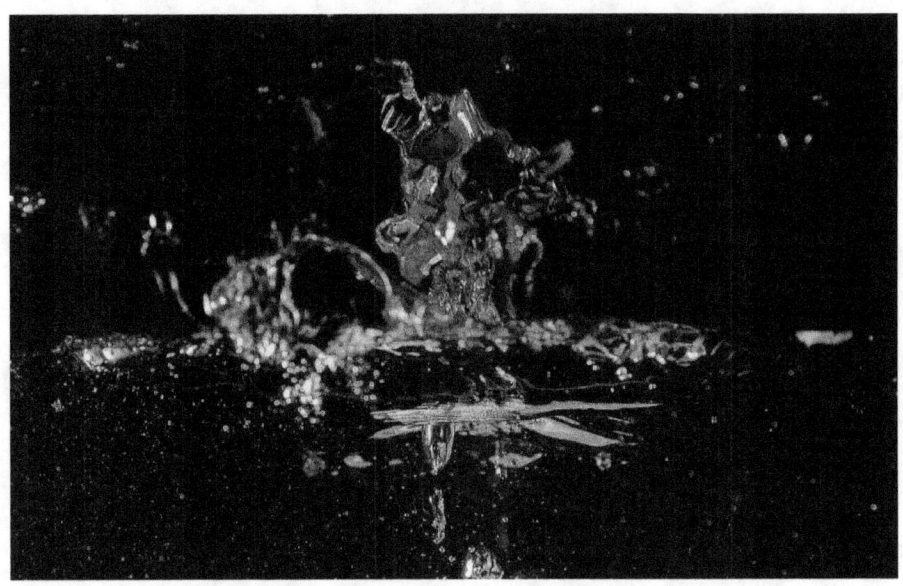

Living with Color Temperature

Color temperature is how "blue" or "red" the light looks to a camera. Indoor light is warm and reddish to the camera, while daylight looks bluer. Our eyes can adjust to these differences so objects don't look too orange indoors or overly blue outside. However, the camera's sensor can detect these variations, so to get accurate colors, we must consider the color temperature when adjusting the camera's color balance, either automatically or manually.

Canon has worked hard to adjust the camera's color balance automatically, but many other tools have been created to help with this, like the ExpoDisc filter. This filter lets the camera measure the light passing through it to set a custom white balance. You can also use a white or gray card for this. When trying to get the exact color temperature for a scene, the main tools are custom white balances using things like the ExpoDisc and adjusting RAW files when importing photos into your image editor.

You only have to worry about color temperature when adjusting the Color Temperature setting in the White Balance section of the Shooting 4 menu. It lets you choose specific color temperatures if you know them. You can also adjust the color balance between blue and amber, magenta and green, and try different white balance options.

Most of the time, you can rely on the "Auto" setting in the Shooting menu's White Balance to adjust the colors properly for your photos. It's a good choice for general situations. However, sometimes, you might want to use preset values or set a custom white balance based on the specific shooting conditions.

If you take photos in RAW format, you can adjust the white balance when you import the image into photo editing software like Photoshop, Photoshop Elements, or Adobe Camera Raw. Color-balancing filters attached to the lens are more suitable for film cameras since the film's color balance cannot be adjusted as much as a digital sensor's.

Daylight

Daylight comes from the sun, and moonlight is sunlight reflected off the moon. Even when the sun is not visible, there is still daylight. Direct sunlight can be very bright and strong, but when it gets scattered by clouds, bounces off objects, or is shaded, it becomes dimmer and less intense.

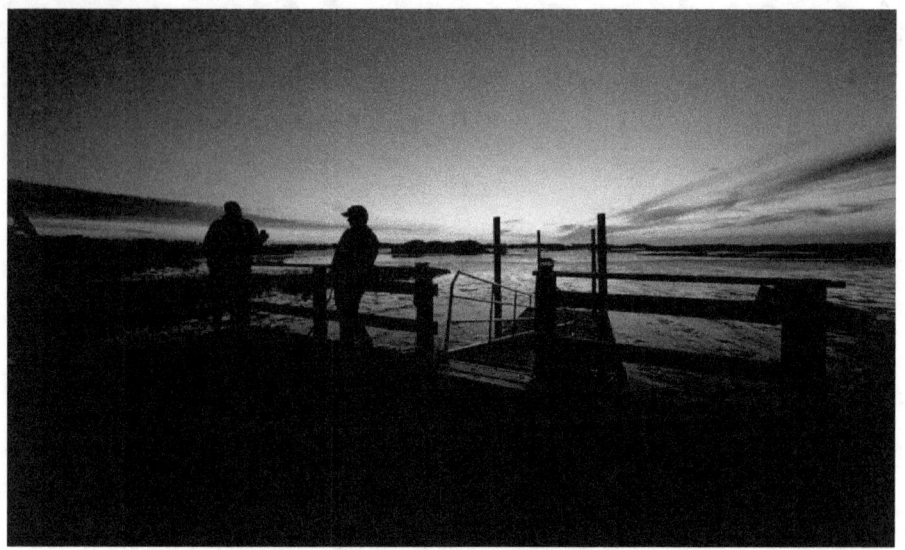

The color of daylight can change throughout the day. At noon, when the sun is directly above us, the light appears bluer because it passes through less air. It is called "high noon," with a color temperature of around 6,000K. During most of the day, the sun is lower in the sky, and the air particles warm the light, giving it a color temperature of about 5,500K. An hour before sunset and an hour after sunrise, the sunlight looks even warmer to our eyes, with a color temperature of 5,000K to 4,500K.

Since you'll be taking lots of photos during the day, it's essential to learn how to handle the brightness, contrast, and color of sunlight in your pictures.

Incandescent/Tungsten/Halogen Light

Tungsten/halogen illumination, or incandescent lights, are modern versions of Thomas Edison's original electric lamp. They have a glass bulb containing a tungsten filament heated by electricity, creating light and heat. These lights are more durable and longer-lasting, using a higher temperature filament housed in a thicker glass filled with halogen gases like iodine or bromine. This higher temperature allows them to produce brighter and whiter light, making them popular for car headlights and photography lighting.

Incandescent lights are not perfect, but they are close enough for photography. Their color temperature can be calculated accurately, so you don't have to worry about color differences, except when the lamp is near the end of its life. The newer types of lights, like compact fluorescent lights (CFL), tungsten, halogen, and eventually LED lights, replace old-style tungsten lamps. LED lights are the future choice for most applications, and factors like contrast depend on the distance of the lamp from the subject and the type of reflectors used.

Fluorescent Light/LEDs

Fluorescent lights are suitable for brightening up spaces, but they have some drawbacks regarding photography. These lights produce visible light without getting too hot because of a chemical reaction. The light they give off can vary depending on the coating and gas used. It can be a problem for photographers because different lamps have different "color temperatures" that are hard to measure precisely. Also, fluorescent lights can miss some colors, making human skin tones look unnatural and eerie. They might lack the warm, reddish tones we usually see in healthy skin and emphasize the cooler blues and greens seen in horror movies.

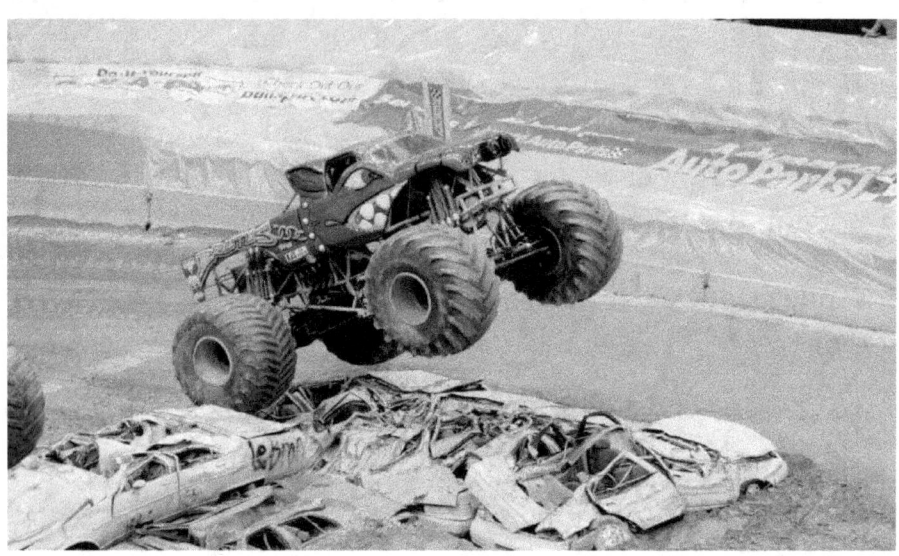

LED lights have become the go-to choice for lighting in various applications, like photography and movie shooting. They have replaced CFLs due to their versatility and convenience. LED lights are now commonly used in movie shooting to fill in shadows and provide continuous light. They are also being adopted in the automotive industry for taillights, headlights, and interior lighting. Some innovations, like the Lume Cube 2, make LED lights even more famous for their brightness and wireless triggering capabilities.

Understanding the White Balance Setting

Using the White Balance setting

It is the first option in the Shooting 4 menu. Suppose the automatic white balance or the preset settings (Daylight, Shade, Cloudy, Tungsten, White Fluorescent, or Flash) don't work well for your situation. In that case, you can customize the white balance using the Custom menu or a specific color temperature value. If you choose the "K" option, you can pick a precise color temperature between 2,500K and 10,000K using the Main dial.

You will only know the exact color temperature of your scene if you have a special tool called a color temperature meter. However, it can still be helpful to know the color temperatures of the preset options when you want to make adjustments by choosing a different color temperature setting. Here are the values used, and two options are available for Auto.

Auto (AWB): Auto white balance adjusts the image's color temperature. It ranges from warm (3,000K) to cool (7,000K). Press the INFO button to switch between Ambience-priority (for warm colors under tungsten light) or White-priority (for neutral whites under tungsten light).

Here are different types of light and their colors:

- **Daylight:** Light from the sun with a color temperature of 5,200K.

- **Shade:** Shady areas with a color temperature of 7,000K.

- **Cloudy:** Light on cloudy days with a color temperature of 6,000K.

- **Tungsten:** Light from tungsten bulbs with a color temperature of 3,200K.

- **White Fluorescent:** Light from white fluorescent bulbs with a color temperature of 4,000K.

- **Flash:** Light from a camera flash with a color temperature of 6,000K.

- **Custom:** Adjustable color temperature ranging from 2,000K to 10,000K.

Color Temperature: The range of color temperatures that can be set between 2,500K and 10,000K in 100K increments.

Picking the correct white balance can significantly change the colors in your picture. The issue with presets like Daylight and Shade is that only six options may be accurate for some situations. However, the good news is that they are usually just slightly off, which might not be noticeable to our eyes. In most cases, Auto or a preset close to the correct white balance should give you satisfactory results.

If you really want to get the colors right or if you often don't like how the colors look using the automatic settings, you can take photos in RAW format and then adjust the color balance later in your photo editing app. Alternatively, you can follow a custom white balance method, which will be explained next.

Creating a custom White Balance setting

You can create your own setting if the camera's automatic white balance or preset settings look wrong. Once you set it up, you can use it anytime you choose "Custom" in the White Balance menu.

To set the white balance correctly for the lighting around you, follow these steps:

1. Focus manually on a plain white or gray object, like a card or wall, using the center spot metering circle in the viewfinder.

2. Take a photo after focusing.

3. Press the MENU button and go to the Shooting 4 menu.

4. Choose Custom White Balance.

5. Rotate the QCD-1 until you see the reference image you just took, then select SET to save it as your Custom setting.

6. Only compatible images for custom white balance will be shown on the screen.

7. Custom white balance images are marked with a custom icon and can't be removed, but you can replace them with a new custom white balance image if needed.

Using an ExpoDisc

Some photographers like to use an ExpoDisc from a company called ExpoImaging. You put a small tool in front of your camera lens to help adjust its white balance. The ExpoDisc comes in different sizes and costs between $75 to $100. Some photographers use a strap to hold the 77mm version before their lens. Others have tried using cheaper alternatives like the lid of a Pringles can. ExpoImaging also makes ExpoCap lens caps with similar features, which you can keep on your lens when you're not taking photos.

There are two types of models: ExpoDisc Neutral and Portrait. The Portrait model is suitable for portraits as it gives a slightly warmer color. For best results, use the product to measure the light falling on your subject, not by pointing the camera directly at the subject but by positioning yourself at the subject's position and pointing the lens towards the light source that will illuminate the scene. Avoid pointing the camera directly at the sun; aim at the sky instead.

I enjoy using the ExpoDisc in two different situations.

Outdoors under mixed lighting: When you take photos outside, you might have different types of light, like sunlight and shade. A custom white balance reading can help you get the right colors when it's difficult to judge with your eyes.

When using studio flash: Many studio flash units change the color of the light when you reduce their power output. For example, if your powerful flash is too bright for your desired photo effect, you can decrease its power, which might alter the light's color temperature. To measure the color temperature, you can use an ExpoDisc, which will likely provide a close enough reading for most studio photographers.

White Balance Bracketing

When using WB bracketing, the camera takes one picture but saves multiple copies of the same image with different color balances. You can adjust the color balance by rotating the Main dial or QCD-1 to the right for more blue/yellow tones or to the left for more magenta/green tones. If you want further adjustments, you can use the multi-controller joystick. Usually, simple changes to blue, yellow, or green tones are enough for most situations.

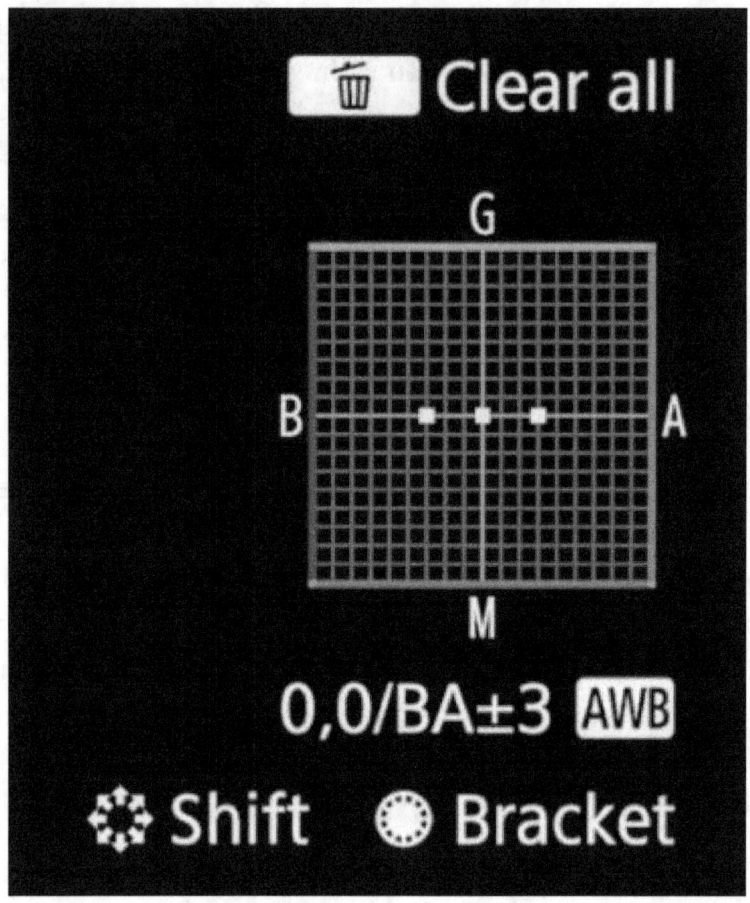

When you see color temperatures named in degrees Kelvin, remember this: lower numbers mean warmer, reddish colors and higher numbers mean cooler, bluer colors. So, 3,400K may sound warmer than 6,000K, but it's the opposite. For a better understanding, imagine a red ember compared to a white-hot welder's torch.

The confusion arises from physics. Scientists use a made-up thing called a black body radiator to calculate color temperature. It's like an object that absorbs all the light that hits it and doesn't reflect any. This black body can also emit light perfectly when heated, but it's not something that exists in the real world. So, it's like a mythical concept.

At a specific temperature, this made-up object always gives off light of the same color. It allows scientists to measure color temperature in degrees Kelvin. For example, incandescent light usually has a color temperature between 3,200K to 3,400K. In comparison, daylight falls within 5,500K to 6,000 K. Different types of lighting used in photography have their color temperature ranges, so we need to be careful when using them.

Taking a Quick Look at Picture Styles

This feature lets you change how your photos look. Picture Styles are settings that fine-tune specific characteristics of your photos, like sharpness, contrast, color richness, and skin tone hue for color images. You can adjust sharpness and contrast for black-and-white photos and apply filter effects or color overlays like sepia, blue, purple, or green tones.

You can choose from different Picture Styles, like Standard, Portrait, Landscape, Fine Detail, Neutral, and Faithful. Additionally, there's an Auto setting and three user-definable options called User Def. 1, User Def. 2, and User Def. 3. You can customize these settings for various types of photography, like sports, architecture, or baby pictures. There's also a Monochrome Picture Style, which lets you modify filter effects or add color toning to black-and-white images.

This scrolling menu has Picture Styles that include six options: Faithful, Monochrome, and three User Def. styles. Picture Styles are very flexible and have preset settings by Canon, but you can customize any of them to your liking. You can even create your styles using the three User Definition files. So, you can make those adjustments if you want vibrant colors like Velvia film, a romantic look with soft colors, or extra contrast for specific weather conditions.

These are different settings for how sharp, colorful, and clear the image appears. These are the names of the features: Sharpness Strength, Sharpness Fineness, Sharpness Threshold, Contrast, Saturation, and Color Tone. Filter Effect and Toning Effect icons appear when you scroll down in the Monochrome Picture Style.

Sharpness: It refers to how clear the edges in a picture appear. When you adjust sharpness, remember that adding too much can cause problems like moiré interference when specific details in the image form a pattern that conflicts with the sensor's pattern. Some softness is necessary to avoid this issue. The default sharpness levels set by Canon aim to minimize moiré, but they sacrifice a bit of sharpness. If you increase sharpness, avoid creating halos around the edges or encountering moiré problems. There are three separate parameters you can adjust in this setting.

- **Strength:** Adjust how much the sharpening effect is applied to your image, ranging from a weak emphasis on outlines (0) to a strong emphasis (7). Be careful not to use too much strength, as it can create a halo and excessive detail around the edges.

- **Fineness:** Choose which edges to sharpen by selecting a value between 1 (sharpen the finest lines) and 5 (sharpen larger, coarser lines). If your image has a lot of fine detail that you want to highlight, use a lower number. For portraits, a higher number might be better to sharpen eyes and hair while avoiding enhancing skin defects. These settings don't affect movie shooting.

- **Threshold:** This is a setting that decides how much to sharpen the edges in a picture. It uses a scale from 1 to 5, where lower numbers sharpen edges even with little contrast, but it can make the picture noisy. Higher numbers only sharpen edges when there's already a lot of contrast, and very high numbers can make the picture look too sharp and unrealistic, like a poster.

Contrast: Contrast is the variation between a photo's dark and bright parts. You can adjust this using the "Contrast" control, which has values ranging from -4 (low contrast) to +4 (higher contrast). Increasing contrast makes the middle tones between the darkest and brightest areas more distinct. Low-contrast settings make the photo look flatter, while high-contrast adjustments can improve the overall tone but might lead to some loss of detail in the dark or bright parts.

Saturation: This is a setting that affects the intensity of colors in a picture. You can make colors look richer and deeper by increasing saturation or lighter and more pinkish by decreasing saturation. However, if you increase saturation too much, some color details may be lost, causing "clipping." It can be detected using RGB histograms.

Color tone: This refers to changing how colors look in a picture. When adjusting it, the biggest impact is on skin tones, making them reddish or yellowish. You can make them redder by reducing the value between 0 and -4 or yellower by increasing the value between 0 and +4.

Filter effect (Monochrome only): It changes how gray tones appear as if the photo was taken with a colored filter. It doesn't add any color to the picture.

Toning effect (Monochrome only): The image toning effect changes the color of a black-and-white photo to sepia, blue, purple, or green while keeping its original shades of gray.

The Picture Styles are preset settings for your photos:

- **Auto:** Makes outdoor scenes look more colorful and vibrant.

- **Standard:** Enhances sharpness and is good for most pictures, except Portrait or Landscape modes.

- **Portrait:** Portrait mode makes colors look more vibrant in portraits, especially for women and children. It also softens the sharpness to make skin texture appear more flattering. The Basic Mode Portrait setting uses this style. If you're taking portraits of men and want a rugged or masculine look, or if you want to emphasize the lines on the faces of older people, you might prefer the Faithful style instead.

- **Landscape:** This style makes blues and greens look more vibrant and sharpens the colors for better landscape photos. It's used in the Basic Zone Landscape mode.

- **Fine detail:** This setting enhances image details with sharpening and contrast but might add some visual noise.

- **Neutral:** This Picture Style offers a less colorful and lower-contrast version of the Standard style. Use it for a more subdued look or when photos are too bright and contrasty, like on a sunny beach day.

- **Faithful:** This style aims to show the colors in your image as close to how the eye sees them.

- **Monochrome:** With this Picture Style, you can take black-and-white photos directly with the camera. If you shoot in JPEG only, the colors are permanently gone. However, if you shoot in JPEG+RAW, you can still get the colors back when importing the RAW files into your image editor, even if you used the Monochrome Picture Style. The screen displays black-and-white images during playback, but the colors are preserved in the RAW file for future use.

CHAPTER 3: CHOOSING BASIC PICTURE SETTINGS

Getting a Handle on Exposure

Exposure in photography is about how much light reaches your camera. It's crucial because it can either make your photo look great by showing all the details and colors, or it can make it look bad by hiding important parts in darkness or washing them out with too much brightness. Getting the right exposure needs some intelligence from the camera or your knowledge.

You may have heard of the "exposure triangle," which involves three main factors: aperture (amount of light the lens lets in), shutter speed (how long the shutter stays open), and ISO sensitivity of the sensor. They work together to create the right exposure for a photo. If you increase the light, you can adjust one of these factors to maintain the same exposure. For example, you can make the aperture larger, increase the shutter speed, or raise the ISO setting. And vice versa, if you decrease the amount of light, you can adjust these factors in the opposite direction to achieve the desired exposure.

Using any of the three camera settings has advantages and disadvantages. Using larger f/stops means less background is in focus, while smaller f/stops give you more focus in the background (but might make the image less sharp). Shorter shutter speeds reduce blur caused by movement, but longer shutter speeds can make motion blur more visible. Higher ISO settings create more visual noise and imperfections, while lower ISO settings reduce these effects.

Exposure is like the brightness and colors in a picture. The essential parts can be too dark or washed out if done wrong. But if it's done right, you'll see all the details you want in the picture. Sometimes, getting the perfect exposure is hard because cameras can only capture some things we see. You might have to decide which details are most important for the photo you want to take, and that's where your creativity comes in.

With digital cameras, it's difficult to capture both bright and dark details in one photo due to the limited range of tones the sensor can handle. To overcome this, photographers use High Dynamic Range (HDR) photography. They combine three different exposures of the same scene using software like Photoshop, Photomatix, or Aurora HDR. These tools can be found at www.hdrsoft.com and www.skylum.com for around $100 each.

To know exposure, you must know how different types of light come together to create a picture. It all starts with the light source, like the sun or a lamp, which travels to your camera through the lens and reaches the sensor that captures the image. Here are the factors we can control that influence exposure.

- **Light at its source:** Our eyes and cameras are most sensitive to visible light, an essential part of photography. Visible light has aspects like color and harshness, determined by the size of the light source. When it comes to exposure, the intensity of the light source is what matters. We can control intensity directly, like adjusting the brightness of an indoor light, or indirectly, using materials that make sunlight appear dimmer.

- **Light's duration:** Most light sources appear constant, but sometimes, the light duration can change quickly, affecting how much light reaches the camera's sensor. For example, a photo's main light comes from a flashing light like an electronic flash.

- **Light reflected, transmitted, or emitted:** After a source creates light, we use it to see and take pictures of objects. The light can come from the objects themselves, be transmitted through them (like from a lit object seen through a translucent material), or be emitted by other sources like candles or television screens. When more or less light is reaching the camera lens from the object, we need to adjust the exposure. We can control this by adding more light sources, using reflectors, or increasing the brightness of the glowing object.

- **The light passed by the lens:** Not all the light that goes towards it passes through it. Filters can remove some light before it goes into the lens. Inside the lens, a part called the diaphragm can change its size to control the amount of light entering the lens. By adjusting the diaphragm, you or the camera's autoexposure system can control the exposure. The size of the diaphragm is referred to as the f/stop.

- **Light passing through the shutter:** After light goes through the lens, the camera's shutter controls how long the sensor gets the light. The shutter can be open for up to 30 seconds or as fast as 1/8000th of a second.

- **Light captured by the sensor:** When light reaches the camera's sensor, not all of it is captured. No information is recorded if the number of photons reaching a specific part of the sensor is too low. On the other hand, if there's too much light, the excess isn't recorded correctly and might affect neighboring areas. We can control the amount of image detail captured by adjusting the ISO setting. Higher ISO settings amplify the incoming light, making the sensor more sensitive.

The exposure of an image depends on various factors: the amount of light produced by the light source, the light reflected or transmitted to the camera, the light passed through the lens, the time the shutter is open, and the sensor's sensitivity. Suppose you change any of these factors, like doubling the available light, increasing the aperture, prolonging the shutter speed, or boosting the ISO setting. In that case, you'll get a corresponding change in the exposure. Likewise, you can increase one factor while decreasing another by a similar amount to maintain the same exposure level.

Correctly Exposed

To calculate the right exposure, they measured the light reflecting from the middle gray patch, which reflects about 12 to 18 percent of the incoming light. The exposure meter in the camera sees this gray patch and thinks it's a middle gray, so it calculates the exposure accordingly. As a result, the patch in the center of the strip appears with the correct brightness, and the black and white patches on the left and right sides also look accurate.

When you take photos with your camera, it tries to make the pictures look good by setting the right brightness. It aims for a middle gray tone to get accurate results. The camera has four different modes to handle challenging situations, like when the subject is backlit or has uneven lighting. I'll explain these modes to you.

Overexposed

The center part shows what happens when the camera measures the exposure based on the darkest black patch on the left side. Since the meter sees less light reflecting from the black patch, it mistakenly tries to make the subject brighter, as if it were a middle gray. As a result, the black patch appears gray, the middle gray patch becomes too bright (light gray), and the white patch on the right loses detail and looks completely white. This overexposure also affects our human subjects, making them appear too bright in the photo.

Underexposed

In simpler terms, the third possibility is that the light meter might mistakenly measure the brightness from the white patch, which is like the subject's blouse, and try to make it look like a middle gray tone. Because the white patch reflects a lot of light, the camera's settings are adjusted to make it darker and look like middle gray. As a result, the originally gray and black patches now appear too dark. To ensure the camera settings are exactly right, it's best to measure the gray patch or use something similar that reflects the same amount of light, like the standard Kodak gray card.

Use a gray card that reflects 12 to 18 percent of the light to get the best exposure in your photos. An evenly illuminated gray card is a good choice for accurate exposure calculations. However, if you use a standard Kodak gray card that reflects 18 percent of light and your camera is calibrated for 12 percent, you'll need to add about one-half stop more exposure than the value metered from the card.

You won't find a mid-tone to measure the correct exposure in very bright scenes, like snowy landscapes or lava fields. Instead of using a gray card, you can use the palm of a human hand (not the backside, as it varies too much). However, remember that a human palm is brighter than a standard gray card. So, you need to increase the exposure by one additional stop. For example, if your meter reading suggests using 1/500th of a second at f/11, you should use 1/500th second at f/8 or 1/250th second at f/11, both of which will give you the same exposure level.

Using Drive Modes and Self-Timer/Remote

Drive modes in your camera are named after the old days of film shooting, where mechanical parts moved the film and delayed the shutter. Your camera has seven drive modes: one for single shots, three for continuous shooting, capturing 3 to 40 frames per second, and three self-timer/remote modes that trigger the shutter after a 10-second or 2-second delay.

To choose a drive mode quickly, use the M-Fn button and locate the Drive icon, the second from the left in the M-Fn array. Highlight it with the QCD-2 and select your desired mode using the Main dial.

- **Single shooting:** When fully pressing the shutter button, the camera captures one picture.

- **High-speed continuous shooting +:** To take photos quickly, press and hold the shutter button. You can typically capture up to 12 shots per second or 40 shots per second with the electronic shutter. However, the speed may vary in certain picture-taking modes.

- **High-speed continuous shooting:** When you keep the shutter button pressed, you can take up to 5.5 pictures per second with the mechanical shutter, 7 pictures per second with the electronic 1st-curtain shutter, or 20 pictures per second with the electronic shutter.

- **Low-speed continuous shooting:** Pressing and holding the shutter button lets you take up to 3 photos per second or 5 photos per second if you use the electronic shutter.

- **Self-timer: 10 sec./remote control:** The camera takes a picture 10 seconds after you press the button to take the photo or use a remote control. It is useful when you want to be in the picture and need time to prepare.

- **Self-timer: 2 sec./remote control:** This version waits for 2 seconds after you press the button to take a picture. It helps to stabilize the camera and reduce shaking when you want to take long exposure shots.

- **Self-timer: Continuous shooting:** After waiting 10 seconds, you can take between 2 to 10 shots. You can set the number of shots on the Quick Control screen or in the Drive mode option under the Shooting menu.

Flash

Flash Exposure Compensation and FE Lock

To lock the flash exposure for a subject not in the center of the frame, use the FE lock button (the * button). First, position the viewfinder to correctly center the subject you want to expose, then press the * button. The camera will calculate the exposure based on a pre-flash. It will remember this correct exposure until you take a picture, and you'll see a lightning bolt with an * in the lower-left corner of the display as a reminder. If you want to recalculate the flash exposure, press the * button again. When you're ready to take the picture, recompose your photo and press the shutter fully.

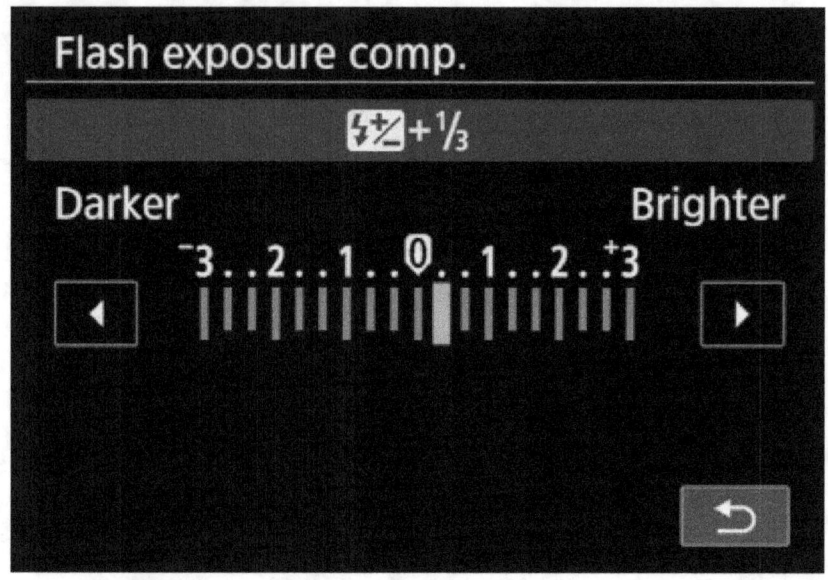

You can adjust the brightness of your photos without using the flash. If you're using specific exposure modes (not Scene Intelligent Auto), you can change the flash settings in four ways.

Set FEC on the flash:

1. Check your Speedlite manual to find out if you can adjust the flash exposure on the flash itself.

2. Look at the sidebar for more information.

3. Remember that if you set flash exposure compensation on the flash, you won't be able to change it using the camera's controls.

Press the INFO button:

1. If you want to see the Shooting Information screen, press the INFO button until it appears.

2. Press the Q button and highlight the FEC icon on the right side of the second row on the Quick Control screen.

3. Use any dial to make the adjustment you want.

Quick Control screen: Once you've opened the Quick Control screen and selected the FEC icon, you can press SET to see a sliding scale displayed at the top right of the screen. You should do this if you prefer using the touch screen for adjustments or need better visibility on the larger screen.

Access External Speedlite Control: To adjust the flash settings on your camera, go to the Shooting 2 menu and press SET.

Choose the Flash Function settings if your camera's flash is connected and turned on. Then, find the Flash Exposure Compensation icon in the second row of the screen and press SET again. It will show a touch-screen sliding scale where you can control the amount of flash illumination.

Remember that flash exposure compensation can work alongside non-flash exposure compensation, allowing you to adjust the amount of light captured from the scene by ambient light while fine-tuning the flash's illumination. The adjustments you make will apply to the subsequent pictures you take, and remember to cancel the flash exposure compensation by reversing the steps when you're finished using it or turning off the camera.

Flash Range

When you use an external flash, the brightness of the flash changes based on three things: how far your subject is, the focal length of the lens, and the ISO sensitivity setting. If your subject is far away, it will receive less light, and the light reduces the farther it is. For example, if your subject is twice as far away, it will only get one-quarter of the light, like two f/stops less light.

Focal length: AA non-zooming flash only lights up a specific area and doesn't change its coverage. If you use a wider lens than the default one, you may have dark areas in the corners of the photo because the frame isn't fully covered. On the other hand, when you zoom in with longer focal lengths, some of the flash's light goes outside the area you want to capture, which is wasteful. External flash units like the 600EX II-RT or EL-1 automatically adjust their coverage to match your lens's zoom setting, directing the flash's light onto the subject you want to capture.

ISO setting: When you increase the ISO sensitivity, the camera captures more light particles called photons. If you double the sensitivity from ISO 100 to 200, it's like making your lens aperture wider from f/8 to f/5.6, which has a similar effect on the brightness of the photo.

Exploring advanced Flash features

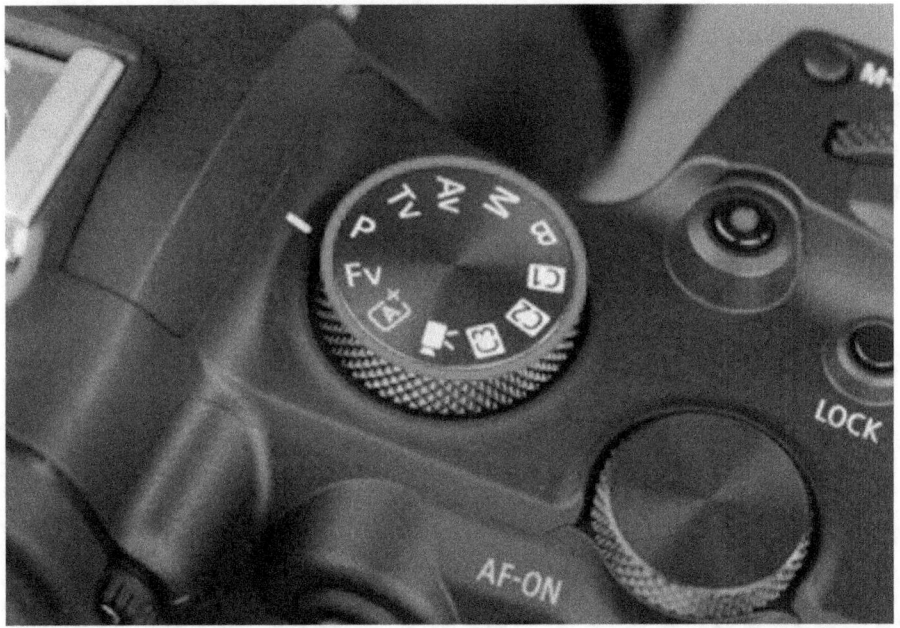

The extra flash is a handy tool to have. Later in the chapter, I'll explain your flash settings in detail. For now, when using specific camera modes like Scene Intelligent Auto, P, Av, Tv, Fv, B, or Manual, attach the flash and turn it on. The way the flash behaves will depend on which mode you choose.

- **Scene Intelligent Auto:** When you set the camera to this mode, the fire will get fired automatically if attached or powered up.

- **Program Mode (P):** The camera takes care of everything automatically, adjusting the flash for fill effects during the day and fully illuminating subjects in low light. It picks a shutter speed and aperture for you.

- **Aperture-priority Mode (Av):** You choose the aperture, and the camera selects a shutter speed based on that. Be careful in this mode because if the camera detects a dark background, it might use the flash to expose the main subject and then keep the shutter open longer to capture the background properly. It can lead to blurry images if you're not using a stabilized lens or a tripod.

  To prevent slow shutter speed with flash, change the Slow Synchro option in the External Speedlite Control menu to 1/200–1/60sec. auto or 1/200sec. fixed. This way, the camera will use faster shutter speeds with flash and avoid blurriness.

- **TV:** When using flash in TV mode, you set the shutter speed from 30 seconds to 1/200th second, and the camera will choose the correct aperture for the correct flash exposure. If you set the shutter speed too high, the camera will automatically lower it to 1/200th second when the flash is on. Again, 1/250th second is available with the electronic first-curtain shutter.

- **Fv:** In Fv mode, you can set the shutter speed, aperture, and ISO sensitivity yourself or let the camera do it automatically. If you don't manually set the shutter speed or aperture when using flash, the camera will act like it's in Program mode. If you only set the shutter speed, it will behave like TV mode; if you only choose the aperture, it will behave like AV mode. If you manually set both the shutter speed and aperture, it will be similar to Manual mode.

- **M/B:** In manual or Bulb exposure modes, you control the shutter speed and aperture settings. When using a flash, the camera will adjust the shutter speed to the sync speed if you try to go faster. The E-TTL II system helps provide the correct exposure for your main subject at the chosen aperture, given that the subject is within the flash's range. In Bulb mode, the shutter remains open as long as the release button or remote control is activated, allowing for long exposures when using the Bulb timer.

CHAPTER 4: TAKING GREAT PICTURES AUTOMATICALLY

Choosing a Focus Mode (AF Operation)

You can easily change the focus on your camera by using the AF/MF selector on the lens. If you're using a semi-automatic shooting mode, you must choose the appropriate focus mode, which Canon calls AF operation. This mode tells the camera when to focus when AF is active.

To set the autofocus mode, go to the Quick Control display on the viewfinder or LCD screen. Look for the AF operation icon, located to the left of the Metering mode icon in the Quick Control screen or second from the top in the left column of the other two views. You can choose between One-Shot or Servo options. If the lens is set to manual focus, these options won't be available, and you'll see an MF indicator.

Your options are:

- **One-Shot:** This mode, sometimes called single autofocus, locks in a focus point when the shutter button is pressed halfway. Green boxes will appear when the image is in focus at the active focus points, or orange boxes if the camera cannot achieve sharp focus. When you press the button or take a picture, the camera will keep the focus steady until you let go of the button or capture the image. This mode works well when your subject isn't moving much.

- **Servo AF:** This mode is like an automatic focus that starts when you press the shutter button halfway. It keeps checking the scene and adjusts the focus if the camera or the subject moves. It's handy for taking pictures of sports or anything in motion.

Selecting AF Area

The Canon EOS R6 II has many focus positions in its sensor for you to choose from. In some shooting modes, the camera automatically selects the focus point based on face detection. In contrast, in other modes, you can let the camera choose the focus point or manually choose it yourself.

There are eight ways to specify the focus point.

- **Spot AF:** You can choose a small autofocus point.

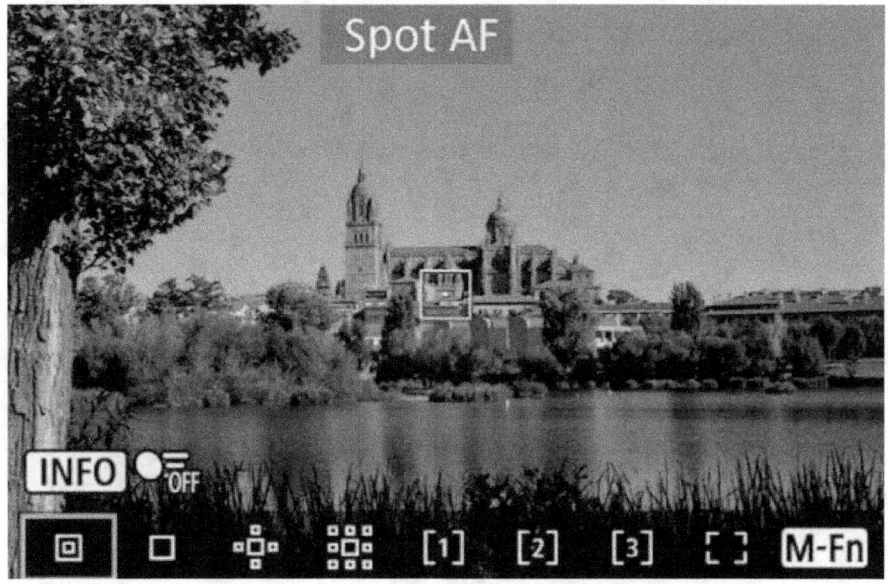

- **1-point AF:** You can choose a slightly larger autofocus point, about three times the size of the Spot AF.

- **Expand AF area:** You can choose a single autofocus point and the four points around it.

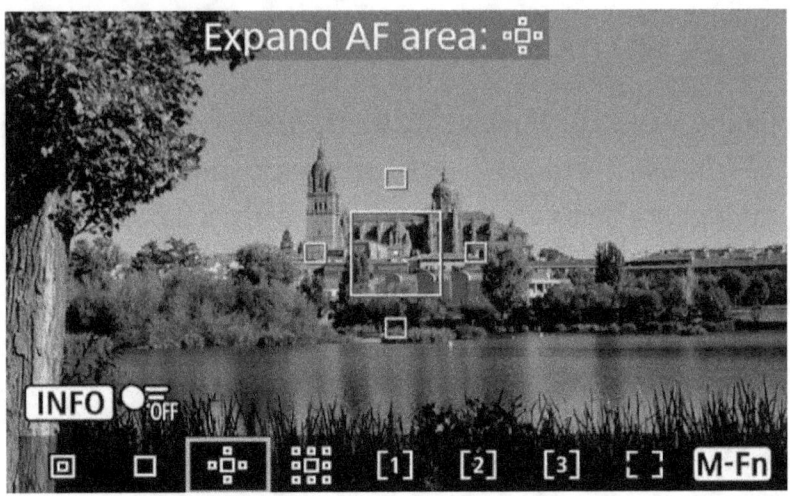

- **Expand AF area: Around.** You can choose a single autofocus point and up to eight points surrounding it.

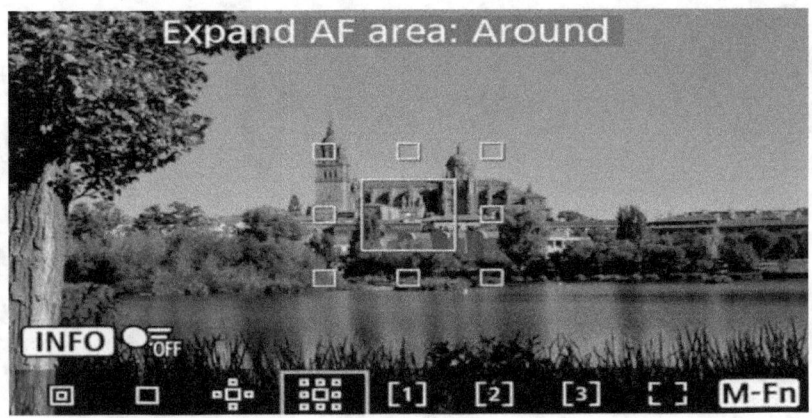

- **Flexible Zone AF 1:** Autofocus points are grouped into square-shaped zones that cover about one-sixth of the frame, and you can select which Zone to use. The camera will try to focus on faces if they are present.

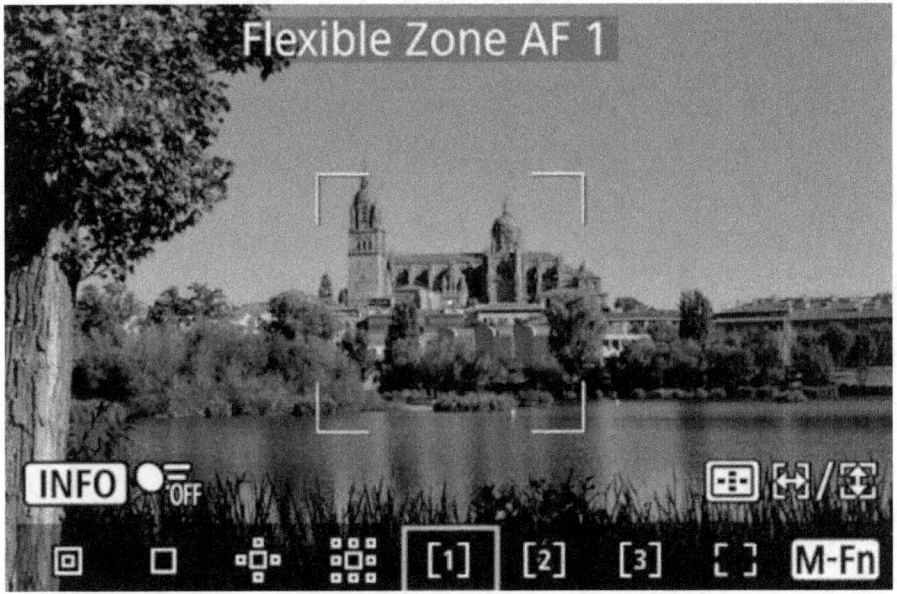

- **Flexible Zone AF 2 (Vertical):** Autofocus points are grouped into larger, vertically oriented zones, and you can select which Zone to use.

- **Flexible Zone AF 3 (Horizontal):** The autofocus points are grouped into a larger horizontally oriented zone that you can specify.

- **Whole Area AF:** The camera dynamically calculates the focusing area based on subject distance, identified people, animals, or vehicles, and subject motion.

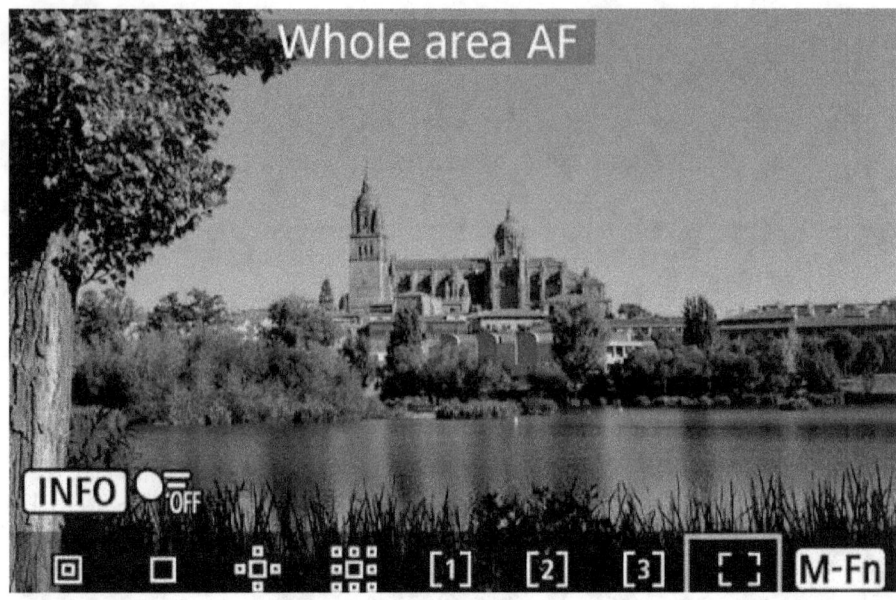

To choose the autofocus areas on your R6 II camera, follow these steps:

1. Press the AF point selection button on the back of the camera, located on the far right.

2. Within about six seconds, press the M-Fn button (located on top of the camera near the shutter release button) repeatedly to cycle through the eight available modes.

3. The display will show each AF area option, and you can select the one you want by highlighting it and pressing the SET button to confirm. Pressing the INFO button, you can also toggle between Whole area or AF points only subject tracking in Servo AF mode.

Exploring Basic Zone Modes

Scene Intelligent Auto Mode

Scene Intelligent Auto is a feature on the R6 II camera that automatically selects the best settings for your photos without you having to do much. Unlike the Program mode, where you can adjust various settings, Scene Intelligent Auto analyzes the scene and chooses the right settings for you based on what it sees. It considers factors like whether your subject is still or moving and then picks the appropriate settings for a better photo.

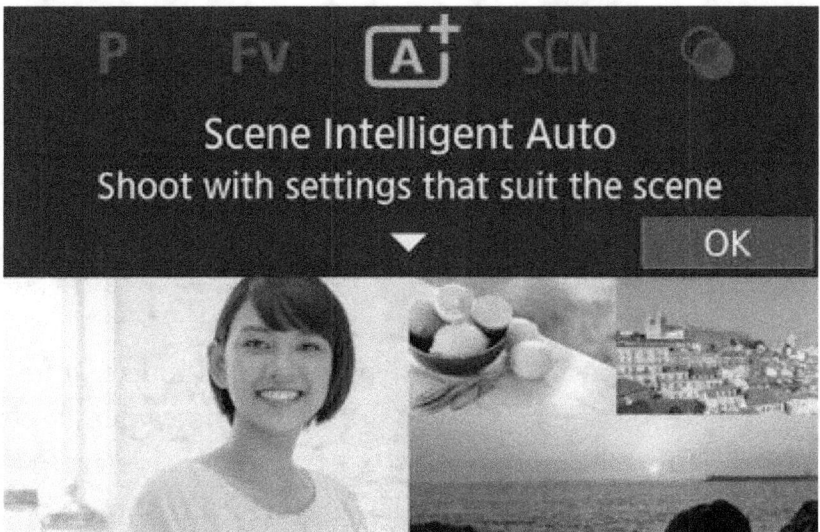

- **ISO speed:** The camera will pick the right ISO setting.

- **Picture Style:** The camera has an "Automatic" Picture Style that's on and picks the right settings for you. But if you changed the Auto Picture Style before, those changes won't apply in Scene Intelligent Auto mode.

- **White balance:** The camera adjusts the colors automatically, and you can't adjust them yourself.

- **Auto Lighting Optimizer:** In Scene Intelligent Auto mode, the camera is always ready and active to capture photos.

- **Color space:** Made to use sRGB colors."

- **Autofocus:** When you press the shutter button halfway, the camera automatically chooses between One-Shot AF (for still subjects) and Servo AF (for moving subjects). You can't manually switch between them. The camera always picks the focus point for you and activates the AF-assist beam when necessary. To turn on or off Eye Detection, press the Q/SET button, highlight the AF Method icon, and press the INFO button.

- **Metering mode:** When you turn the Mode dial to the A+ position, a screen will appear on the camera. Select "OK" to see another view on the touch screen. In the upper-left corner, you'll see an icon showing the camera's chosen scene mode (e.g., Portrait). On the left side are icons for the settings you can adjust using the touch screen.

- **Image quality/size:** Tap the icon to choose between different image sizes like RAW, JPEG, and others, and also to select the movie recording size.

- **Drive mode:** Tap the icon to select different shooting options: taking a single photo, capturing three continuous shots at different speeds, setting a self-timer with delays of 2 or 10 seconds, or using a continuous self-timer that takes multiple shots after the timer runs out.

- **Touch Shutter (Enable/Disable):** When Touch Shutter is on, you can tap on someone's face or something else in the picture, and it will take a photo.

- **Manual focus:** Apart from the three options mentioned earlier, you can select Manual focus using the AF/MF switch on the camera's front or the lens (if it has one).

- **Creative Assist:** In the bottom-right corner of the screen, you'll find the lens's focal length/zoom setting and an icon that allows you to use Creative Assist.

The reason it's called Scene Intelligent mode is because the camera can accurately guess if your subject belongs to a specific category like Special Scene (which I'll talk about soon). It will then automatically apply that Scene mode as if you had selected it yourself. You'll see an icon showing the chosen scene in the top-left corner of the display.

In Scene Intelligent Auto mode, you can choose:

71

1. **Manual focus:** Change focus by using the AF/MF switch on the lens.

2. **Touch focus:** Tap on a person's face or another subject on the touch screen when Continuous AF is disabled.

3. **Drive mode:** Use the Quick Control screen to select single shooting, continuous shooting (high/low-speed), silent single shooting, silent continuous shooting, or 10 sec./2 sec. self-timer modes.

4. **Image quality/size:** Press the Q button to pick between RAW, JPEG, and other image size options, including Movie Recording Size. Shooting menu options are also accessible from the truncated four-tab menu system, along with two Autofocus menu tabs.

Creative Assist

Scene Intelligent Auto has a Creative Assist feature that works like the one in Playback mode. It allows you to add special effects to your photos as you take them. To use it with A+ mode, tap the Creative Assist icon at the lower right on the touch screen or press the Q/SET button.

There are icons on the app representing different presets and settings that you can use.

Presets: The first set of icons shows 11 preset effects like Vivid, Soft, Warm, Cool, Green, Shine, Lime, Peach, B&W, Blue, and Purple.

Settings: The second set of icons has seven settings: Background Blur, Brightness, Contrast, Saturation, Color Tone 1, Color Tone 2, and Monochrome. You can adjust each setting individually; for example, you can change the Background Blur from Blurred to Auto to Sharp and Brightness from Darker to Brighter. Color Tone 1 and Color Tone 2 can add specific colors like Blue or Amber bias and Magenta or Green bias, respectively. Monochrome allows you to add black-and-white, sepia, blue, purple, or green hues to your scene.

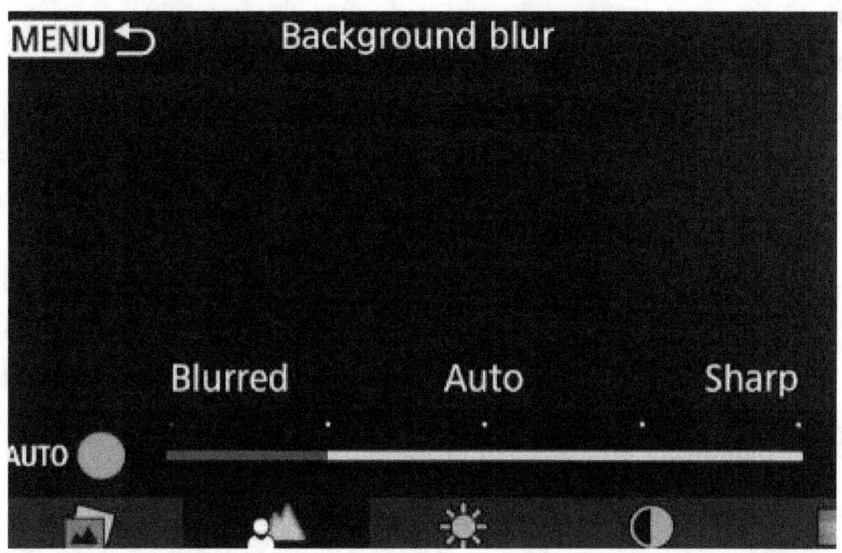

Any settings you've adjusted will be lost when you change shooting modes or turn off the camera. To keep those adjustments for the future, go to the Shooting 4 menu and enable "Retain Creative Assist Data" when the Mode dial is set to SCN. Then, press the INFO button on the settings screen to save those adjustments as Presets. You can save up to three sets labeled User 1, User 2, and User 3. If all three slots are filled, you must overwrite one to save a new set.

The Creative Assist options allow you to change the look of your image in different ways, like adjusting brightness, contrast, colors, and background blur (depth-of-field). But remember, you can't use Background Blur with electronic flash.

Special Scene Mode on the camera can be accessed through the SCN position on the Mode dial. It offers 13 subject categories, covering various common things you might want to photograph. If you activate the Mode Guide, a helpful screen will guide you in choosing a Scene mode. Otherwise, you can press the Q button and use the Main dial to cycle through the available Scene modes. Your available options are:

- **Portrait:** This mode makes the background blurry and prevents shaky images using larger openings and faster shutter speeds. If you keep the shutter button pressed, the R6 II will take many photos in a row, which is excellent for catching quick expressions in portraits. Skin tones and hair look smoother and more attractive.

- **Group Photo:** To get better pictures, use a wide-angle lens. It helps keep everything focused, so people in the front and back of a group will be sharp and clear in your photos.

- **Landscape:** The R6 II camera aims to achieve more focus on the subject by using smaller f/stops, resulting in a clearer background. It also enhances colors to make

74

them look more vibrant. The camera's flash is turned off, but if you attach and activate an external Speedlite, it will fire and provide additional light.

- **Panoramic Shot:** You can make a wide picture by turning the camera while taking the photo and following the instructions on the screen.

- **Sports:** In this mode, the R6 II camera tries to capture fast-moving moments by using quick shutter speeds, takes multiple pictures with just one button press, and continuously adjusts focus as your subject moves.

- **Kids:** This mode helps you take clear pictures of active kids by continuously focusing on their movements and capturing a series of photos. The camera adjusts skin tones to make them look lively and healthy. Place the AF point on your main subject, press the shutter halfway, and the camera will follow the child's motion. You'll hear a beep when it refocuses, and if it can't focus properly, a blinking indicator will show in the viewfinder.

- **Panning:** This mode makes moving objects look blurry by using a slow shutter speed while you turn the camera to follow them. It gives a sense of motion to the photo.

- **Close-Up:** This mode is like Portrait mode, but it focuses on close-up subjects with a blurry background and reduces shaky photos when you get close. If your camera is on a tripod or has image stabilization, you can use Aperture-priority (Av) mode for more control over the depth of field with a smaller f/stop.

- **Food.** In this mode, your food pictures will look bright and delicious because they enhance the colors and contrast.

- **Night Portrait:** This mode uses flash and natural light to create a photo. The flash mainly lights up the subject, while the available light exposes the background. To do this, longer exposure times are needed, so it's essential to use a tripod, monopod, or IS lens for stability.

- **Handheld Night Scene:** In this mode, the R6 II camera takes four pictures one after the other and puts them together to create a clear photo with less blur from shaky hands.

- **HDR Backlight Control:** The R6 II camera captures three pictures at different brightness levels and combines them to create one photo with better details in bright and dark areas.

- **Silent Shutter:** It takes a picture quietly using the electronic shutter instead of the noisy mechanical one.

Creative Filters

The R6 II camera has a cool feature called Creative Filters that you can use while taking pictures. Using the Playback Creative Filters option, you can also use these filters on photos you've already taken. Using the filters while taking the photo lets you see how they will look in real-time. But if you apply them to a photo you've already taken, the original image will remain unchanged, and the modified version will be saved separately. You can use these filters with the optical viewfinder and the live view with the LCD screen. However, you won't be able to preview the effects beforehand when using the optical viewfinder.

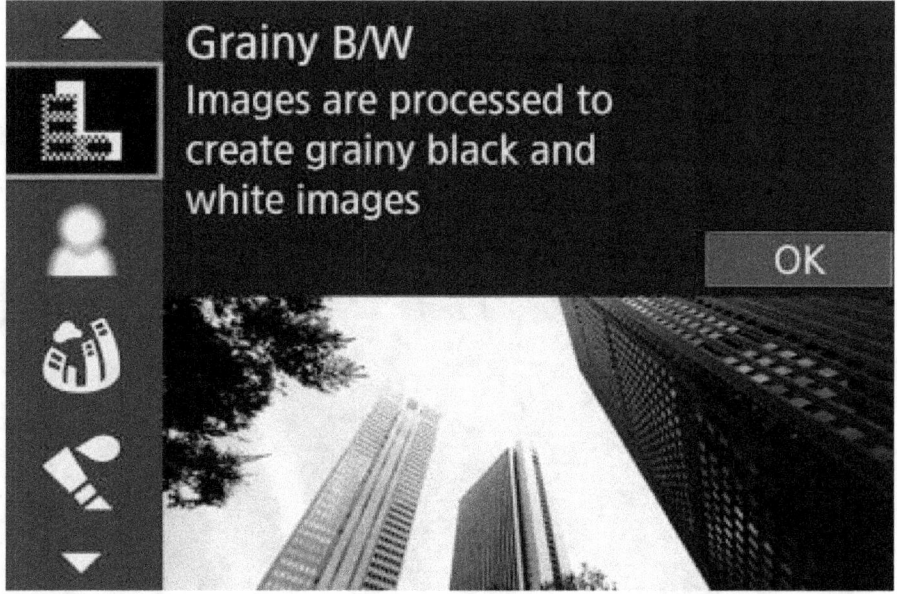

To use creative filters on your camera, turn the Mode dial to the Creative Filters position, located between the SCN and C1 positions. If the Mode Guide is on, press the SET button, and you can choose from a list of filters like Grainy B/W, Soft Focus, Fish-eye Effect, Water Painting Effect, Toy Camera Effect, and HDR Art (Standard, Vivid, Bold, and Embossed). If the Mode

Guide is off, press the Q button and use the Main dial to select a filter from the Quick Control screen.

Each filter can be adjusted. For five filters, you can modify the effect by pressing the up directional button and using left/right controls to increase/decrease parameters. For example, with Grainy B/W, you can adjust the contrast; with Fish-eye, the Strength of the effect; with Water Painting, the Color Density; and with Toy Camera, you can choose between Warm, Neutral, and Cool color tones. All filters, except the four HDR choices, allow you to specify Drive mode and Built-in Flash controls. (The HDR modes only allow Drive mode changes.)

CHAPTER 5: CAPTURING VIDEO

Movie Shooting 1 Menu

Movie Recording Size

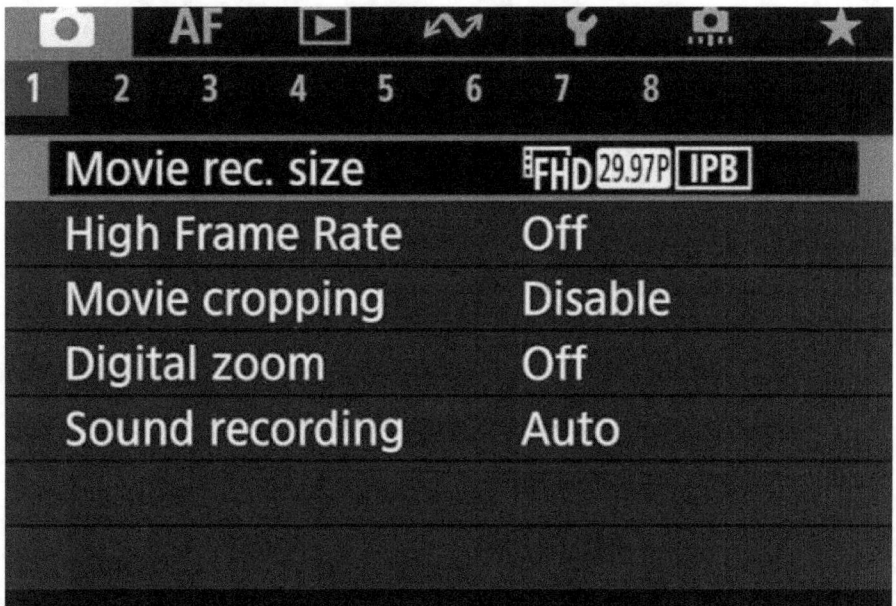

This is the first option in the Movie Shooting 1 menu. Your camera has many video recording quality settings, including very clear 4K video. In short, you have different choices to pick from.

- **Image size:** The Movie comes in two resolutions: 4K and Full HD. The resolution and size may change based on the recording quality and movie crop settings.

- **Frame Rate:** This is about how many pictures or parts of pictures are taken every second. Commonly, it's shown as 120 pictures per second, 60 pictures per second, 30 pictures per second, and 24 pictures per second (in NTSC mode used in North America, Japan, and other countries). The rates in Europe and other areas using the PAL specification are different: 100 pictures per second, 50 pictures per second, and 25 pictures per second. The actual number of frames per second is slightly less than the stated value, and I'll explain why below.

- **Compression Method:** To save space and ensure videos can be stored easily, each video frame is compressed using ALL-I or IPB formats. If you see an icon with a downward-pointing arrow, it means the video has a lower bit-rate capture.

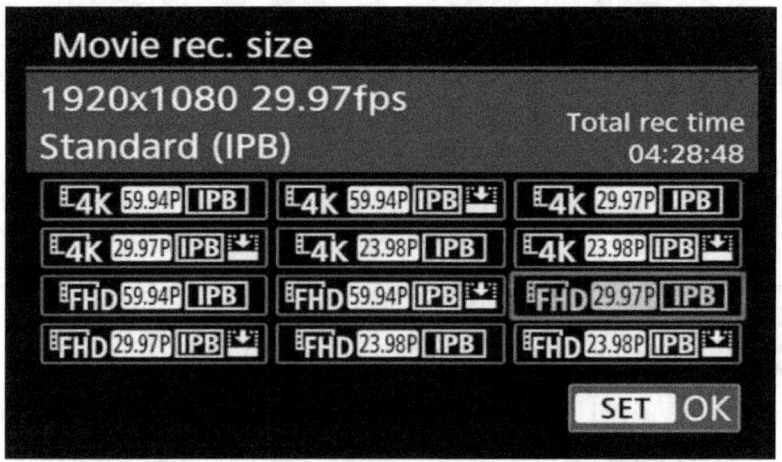

All movies are stored using the MP4 format, which is a standard and widely supported video file container. The videos are recorded using the MPEG4 AVC/H.264 codec, and the files receive the .MP4 extension.

High Frame Rate

When you turn on Frame Rate movies, your video is recorded at a very high speed and then played back at a slower speed, creating slow-motion effects. The slow motion can be 6 times slower for NTSC videos or 4 times slower for PAL videos. If you use the camera's HDMI port to view the video, it will be displayed 2 times slower.

High Frame Rate videos don't capture sound and have a maximum duration of 1 hour and 30 minutes. They may show flickering under specific lighting, and the ISO speed settings are limited to specific ranges. This feature is excellent for creating slow-motion action scenes or analyzing movements in your videos.

It lets you capture videos that play back at either 1/4 or 1.6 times the normal speed. While not slow enough to analyze small details like flaws in a golf swing, it can still add a cool effect to your videos, like those Baywatch-style running sequences you might see in a parody of Dwayne Johnson or David Hasselhoff.

The cool feature has its downsides. Your video quality will be at Standard HD (1280 × 720) resolution and without sound. You can only record for a maximum of 7 minutes and 29 seconds, which should be enough for most uses; longer slow-motion clips would be tough to watch. Autofocus is unavailable, and the high frame rate makes digital IS useless.

The secret to slow-motion is that the video is recorded at lower resolutions (180p/120p for NTSC, 150p/100p for PAL) and then played back at 30/25 fps, making each frame display for 6X or 4X longer than it was captured. The results are good, but there might be flickering under fluorescent or LED lighting and oddities when using HDMI output. Time codes won't be recorded when Count Up is set to Free Run. Canon suggests checking the Movie Recording Size Setting after turning off the High Frame Rate video.

Movie Cropping

When recording videos, the full image captured by the camera sensor is always trimmed to some degree. Because the video has a different shape (16:9) compared to still photos (3:2), parts from the top and bottom of the frame are cut off to fit the video's aspect ratio. Additionally, depending on your video mode and lenses, more of the remaining area might be cropped. This setting allows you to have some control over how the image is cropped in your videos.

Your options are:

- **Movie Cropping: Disable:** This mode works well with RF-mount and EF-mount lenses, which are the usual full-frame lenses when connected using an adapter.

- **Movie Cropping: Enable:** With this setting, your video will always be cropped, and the visible area will be the same as when using Canon APS-C lenses with the RF-S or EF-S designation. The green box represents the cropped area. Please note that you won't be able to capture High frame-rate movies with the R6 II when using RF-S or EF-S lenses or when Movie Cropping is enabled. Additionally, there's a slight extra crop when using Movie Digital IS.

Digital Zoom

When you set your Movie Size to specific options like FHD 29.97, 23.98 (NTSC), or FHD 25 (PAL), you can use a digital zoom feature that magnifies the image up to 10 times. This zoom takes pixels from the sensor's center, making them bigger to fill the movie frame. However, because it crops the image, it can make the picture look noisier and reduce its quality. When using this zoom, the live view while shooting might appear grainy. The feature works with any lens, even fixed focal length prime lenses.

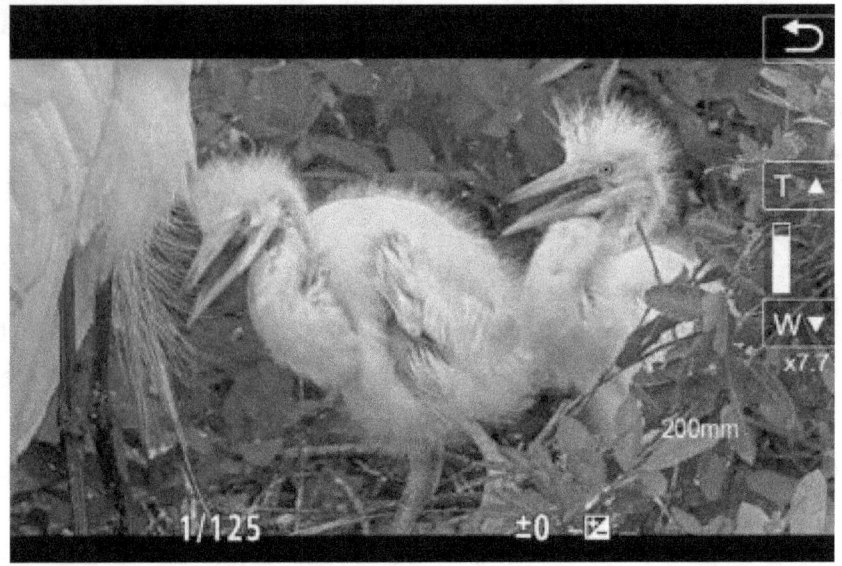

To activate the zoom, you can tap the W/T icon on the lower-right corner of the LCD screen. It's a good idea to assign a button for zoom activation using the Customize Buttons option in the Custom Functions 3 menu. This way, you can zoom while viewing the viewfinder without using the LCD screen. Once the zoom is active, you can zoom in and out using the multi-controller joystick.

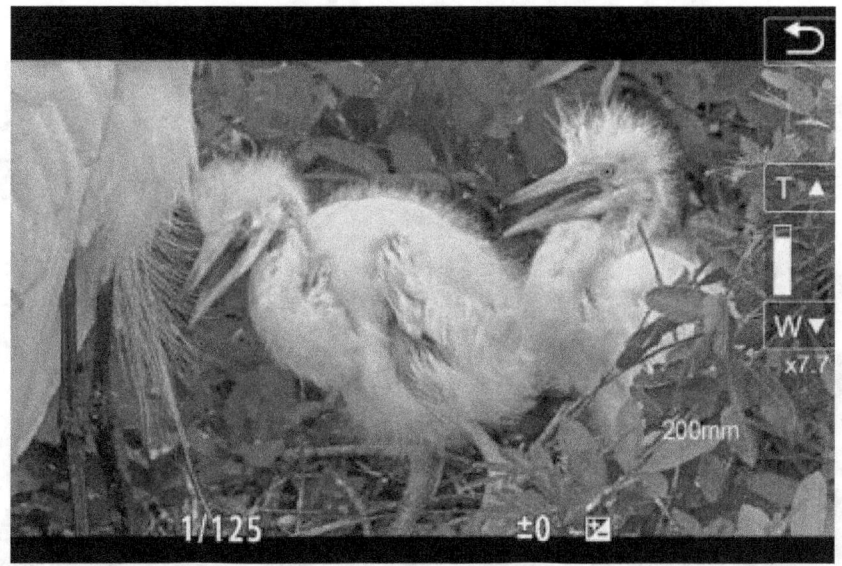

To avoid blurry photos on the R6 II camera, consider using a tripod to zoom in digitally at 200mm or higher distances. Digital zoom may limit features like ISO speed, time-lapse movies, creative filters, and magnified view. Additionally, it can make the camera sensor heat up faster, leading to shorter recording times.

Sound Recording

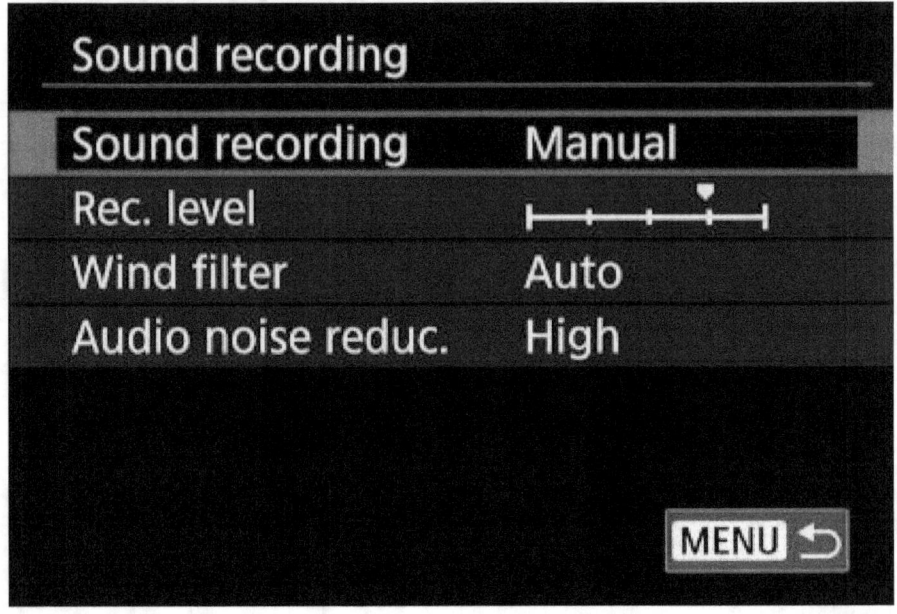

You can pick how the sound is recorded - either automatically, manually, or not at all. You can also turn on or off a filter to reduce wind noise and adjust the audio noise reduction to make it quieter. In the Movie Scene Intelligent Auto mode, you can choose between automatic recording and no sound. However, you can't adjust the left/right balance.

- **Auto:** The audio level is set for you.

- **Manual:** You can pick from 64 sound levels. Adjust the Rec Level by turning the QCD-1 while looking at the decibel meter at the bottom of the screen. Aim for an average of -12 dB for the loudest sounds. Be careful not to reach the 0 point on the scale, as it will distort the recording.

- **Disable:** First, record the video without any sound. Then, you can add voices, music, or other sounds to your video using movie editing software. If you're connected to another device, like a recorder with HDMI, ensure the camera's sound recording is enabled to hear the sound during recording.

- **Wind Filter:** You can turn on a setting to reduce wind noise and low tones in the sound recording. If wind isn't an issue, you'll get better audio quality by turning off this setting. You can use an external microphone with a windshield for even better results.

- **Audio Noise Reduction:** This setting helps reduce unwanted sounds from lens motors and background noise so you can capture clearer audio. However, be aware that it might make other background sounds more noticeable since the white noise won't cover them anymore.

You can use the microphone in the camera or connect a separate one using the jack on the left side. An external microphone is better because the built-in one might pick up camera noises like the autofocus motor. Headphones are handy for monitoring sound. To adjust the headphone volume, press the Q button, choose Headphone, and turn the Main dial.

Movie Shooting 2 Menu

Movie ISO Speed Settings

'📹ISO speed settings

ISO speed	
ISO speed range	100-25600
Max for Auto	25600
✳️Max for Auto	25600
	MENU ↰

It is the first of only two movie settings in the Movie Shooting 2 menu. It lets you choose ISO parameters for movie shooting, like selecting a specific ISO speed or setting limits for the camera to choose in Auto ISO mode. There are some differences from the Still photography settings in this menu.

- **Manual ISO settings:** When using the camera in Manual exposure mode, you can pick the ISO value you want. But if you switch to other exposure modes like Av, TV, P, or TV, the camera will automatically set the ISO for you.

- **No Auto Range:** In Movie mode, you can't pick a set of ISO numbers for Auto ISO. You can only select the highest ISO value that the camera will use.

- **Maximum ISO:** You can choose the highest ISO settings for regular and time-lapse videos.

- **Cannot set Minimum Shutter Speed:** When making videos, the speed at which the camera takes pictures has an important role. It can affect how the video looks if the speed is too slow or too fast. Unlike the photo mode, you can't select a minimum speed to increase the camera's sensitivity to light.

- **ISO Speed:** In simple terms, when you use the automatic modes (A+, P, Av, and TV) in the Movie Scene Intelligent Auto setting of your camera, the ISO is automatically set between ISO 100 and ISO 25,600. However, switching to Manual exposure mode allows you to choose a specific ISO speed between ISO 100 and ISO 25,600. Additionally, in Manual mode, you can extend the ISO range to include ISO 51,200, ISO 102,400, or ISO 204,800 by using the ISO Speed Range setting. Surprisingly, Manual mode also has an Auto setting, which means that even though you manually set the shutter speed and aperture, the camera will adjust the ISO to achieve the correct exposure automatically.

- **ISO Speed Range:** You can choose the lowest and highest ISO settings.

- **Minimum:** You can adjust the minimum sensitivity of the camera from ISO 100 to ISO 12,800. Even if you enable Highlight Tone Priority in the settings, the maximum sensitivity will stay at 12,800.

- **Maximum:** You can choose ISO settings ranging from ISO 51,200 to ISO 204,800, but remember that they are marked with an "H" to indicate they are expanded options. The Highlight Tone Priority setting won't affect these ISO settings.

- **Max for Auto:** This acts as a "safety net" for Auto ISO. It ensures the highest ISO setting is controlled.

- **Time-lapse Max for Auto:** Choose the highest sensitivity setting for shooting time-lapse videos in 4K or Full HD. The default is 12,800, but you can pick any value between 400 and 25,600.

HDR Movie Recording

It is the only extra option in the Movie Shooting 2 menu that you can use only in Movie mode. This option controls whether to record movies with HDR (High Dynamic Range) or not. There are no other settings you need to adjust for this. However, remember that other settings like Highlight Tone Priority, Canon Log, Movie Digital IS, and Movie Cropping must be turned off if you want to use HDR shooting. The movie quality for HDR recording is set at FHD 29.97P IPB.

Movie Shooting 3 Menu

Av 1/8-stop Increments

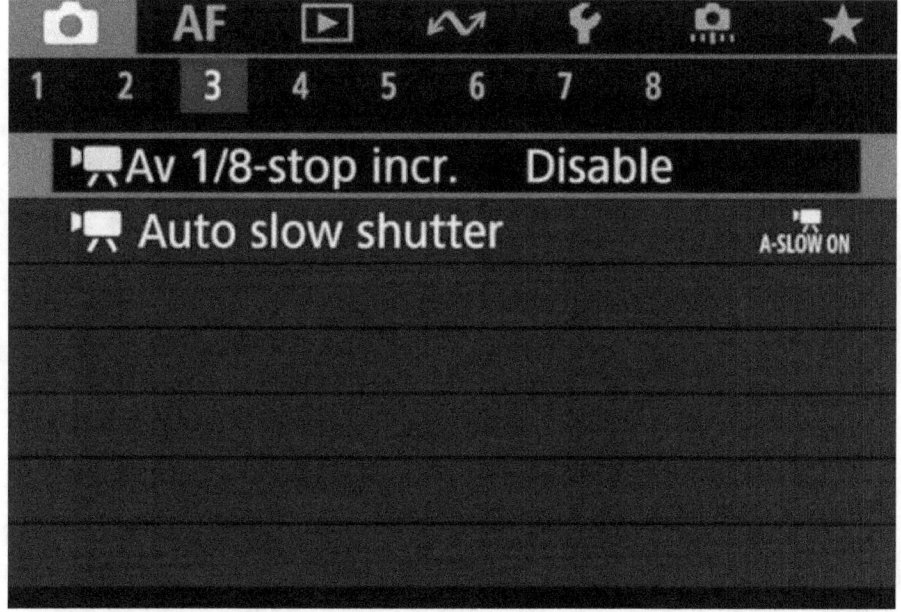

It is the first of only two options in the Movie Shooting 3 menu. RF-mount lenses have more precise aperture control compared to EF/EF-S lenses. Canon allows adjusting f/stops in smaller steps of 1/8th stop, which is useful for consistent exposure while shooting movies. This feature is available in the Av and M modes, where you have full control over the aperture. You can enable this option to select 1/8th-stop increments instead of larger 1/2 or 1/3-stop jumps that might be set in Custom Functions 1's Exposure Level Increments entry. Note that this feature won't work with EF or EF-S lenses.

Movie Auto Slow Shutter

Use this option to let the camera choose a slower shutter speed up to 1/30th of a second when taking photos with Program or Aperture-priority mode at a frame rate of 60p. The feature can be turned either on or off.

- **Disable:** If you shoot video in Program and Av exposure modes with a frame rate of 1/60th second or faster, the video will look smoother and more natural, and each frame will be clearer due to the higher shutter speed. But in low light, the video might look darker than usual.

- **Enable:** Slower shutter speeds, like 1/30th second, can make videos look better and less grainy, as they allow a lower ISO setting. However, moving objects might appear blurry or leave a visible trail due to the longer exposure.

Movie Shooting 4 Menu

Canon Log Settings

Canon Log, or C-log3, is a feature in a camera's Movie Shooting 4 menu that helps capture videos with a wide range of colors and details. It initially makes the video look flat and low-contrast, but this is improved during editing to create a high-quality video. The basic Canon Log profile allows a significant increase in dynamic range, and it also has a "View Assist" function to preview a corrected version before editing.

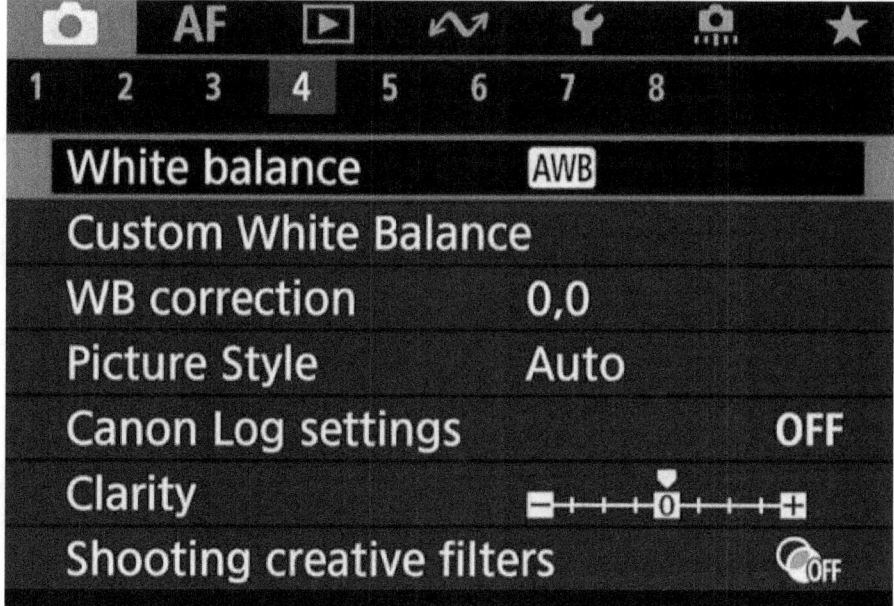

C-log uses specific data processing techniques to evenly distribute the captured data and desaturate colors, making it easier to correct and enhance the video later. It provides videographers with 10 "look-up tables" to correct gamma and color space when viewing the video on an external monitor.

The latest version, C-log3, offers more advantages over the original C-log, such as a higher base ISO rating, better handling of highlights and shadows, and improved compatibility with Canon's Cinema EOS models.

Canon Log settings	
Canon Log	On (C.LOG3)
View Assist.	On
Characteristics	0, 0, 0
Color space	BT.709

MENU ↰

To capture movies with Canon Log, follow these simple steps:

1. Use Manual exposure by changing the Movie Shooting mode to Manual.

2. Go to Canon Log Settings in the Movie Shooting 4 menu.

3. Select Canon Log: On -- C.LOG3 for 10-bit video recording to the internal memory card or an external recorder. To turn off Canon Log, choose Off.

4. Optionally, set View Assist to get a clearer display on the camera's LCD screen for C-Log videos, but it won't affect the video files.

5. Adjust Characteristics like Sharpness, Strength, Saturation, or Hue using sliders for Canon Log video.

6. Choose BT.709, BT.2020, or Cinema Gamut as your color space for HDMI output.

7. Adjust ISO speed, shutter speed, and aperture settings.

8. Start recording your video on the internal memory card or an external video recorder.

Movie Shooting 6 Menu

Pre-recording Settings

▢	AF	▶	↝	⚙		▢	★
1	2	3	4	5	6	7	8	

Pre-recording set.	Off
Time-lapse movie	Disable
Movie self-timer	Off

The Movie Shooting 5 menu has no movie-specific options. So, I'll ignore it. The Movie Shooting 6 menu has three video-oriented options. One of them lets your camera start recording a few seconds before you press the capture button. This way, you won't miss any important action, like when you want to capture something cute a toddler is doing. When your camera is on Standby in Movie mode, it's already creating a video signal, so it's easy to include the last 5 or 3 seconds of footage (you can choose) in the video you capture. This extra time can be helpful when you edit the video later.

Time-lapse Movie

Time-lapse movie	FHD 29.97P IPB
Time-lapse	Enable
Interval	00:00:03
No. of shots	0300
Movie rec. size	FHD
Auto exposure	Fixed 1st frame
🎥 00:11:57	▶ 00:00:15
	MENU ↩

Time-lapse photography is for more than just nature photographers who want to show the miracle of a flower bud gradually opening to its full blossoming glory. Time-lapse is becoming very popular in movies and TV shows. It shows time passing quickly like the sun moving across the sky during the day or the changing seasons. Canon allows you to use this technique, too.

- **Time-lapse Movie:** To set up, click Enable or Disable to turn off the option.

- **Interval:** You can choose how long to wait between each shot, from a few seconds to nearly 100 hours.

- **Number of Shots:** Enter how many shots you want for the sequence, anywhere from 2 to 3,600. The estimated total time for the whole sequence will be displayed at the bottom of the screen. If the playback time is shown in red, it means the memory card doesn't have enough space, or your settings will create a file larger than 4GB (don't worry; SDXC cards are automatically formatted in the camera in exFAT, only SDHC cards or cards not formatted in the camera are affected). The recording will stop when the card is full, or the maximum file size is reached.

- **Movie Recording Size:** Depending on the region, You can choose between 4K (29.97P or 25.00P) or FHD (29.97P or 25.00P).

- **Auto Exposure Setting:** You have two options for metering when shooting:

- **Fixed 1st Frame:** The exposure is set based on the first shot and remains the same for all subsequent shots. Use this when you want constant exposure, even if the lighting changes.

- **Each Frame:** Metering is done separately for each shot in the sequence. It's useful for time-lapse shots of a city skyline from dawn to dusk, as it adjusts the exposure for each stage of the day.

You can adjust the screen auto-off settings. You can either turn off automatic dismissal (the screen will turn off after about 30 minutes) or enable it to turn off the screen 10 seconds after shooting begins, giving you time to check your framing and exposure.

You can also turn on or off the "Beep Per Exposure Taken" feature, which provides feedback for each shot. The electronic shutter is silent, but this feature allows you to select the volume level for the beep sound.

Movie Self-timer

This feature lets you delay the start of recording a movie for either 10 or 2 seconds. It gives you time to get ready in front of the camera (choose 10 seconds if you need more time, like combing your hair; 2 seconds if you're ready to go). If you don't have a remote control, you can use this setting to avoid shaky footage after pressing the Movie button with your finger. Vloggers might find it helpful for spontaneous videos, but serious R6 II users who are good at editing may not need it to fix rushed scenes.

CONCLUSION

The Canon EOS R6 II is a powerful and versatile camera that is capable of producing stunning images and videos. It is a great choice for photographers and videographers who demand the best performance.

To get the most out of the Canon EOS R6 II, it is important to understand its key features and how to use them. Hence, this book is your best bet.

In this user guide, I discussed some of the key features of the Canon EOS R6 II and how they can be used to take stunning photos and videos. I also provided some tips for getting the most out of the camera.

www.ingramcontent.com/pod-product-compliance
Lightning Source LLC
Chambersburg PA
CBHW062347290526
45794CB00005B/2126